Pilgrim Writers

———

ANTHOLOGY

·THE FIRST TEN YEARS·

HAMBLETT HOUSE

ISBN: 978-0-9661049-3-6

Published by Hamblett House LLC, P.O. Box 50411, Nashville, TN 37205

Manuscript Editors: Sheri Malman and Amy Lyles Wilson
Proofreader: Eve Hutcherson

Design and Production: Lane Goddard and Bruce Gore
Cover design: Bruce Gore

With thanks to Jen Chesak, www.wanderinginthewordspress.com, and Lynn Marie Houston, lynnmhouston.com.

"It's the sharing of our stories that saves us."

—AMY LYLES WILSON

CONTENTS

PREFACE

I have long cared for words: the way they sound, what they might mean, all they can do. Their ability to inform, to inspire, and, most importantly, the wondrous way they can—if written with heart and heard with compassion—remind people they are not alone.

As we were growing up, my father—the first love of my life— taught my two sisters and me to remember our fellow pilgrims as we made our way through life. We watched our parents care for one another, for us, and for the community at large. And I see life as a pilgrimage of sorts, a meandering full of wonder and struggle, curiosity and challenge, joy and heartbreak. Hence Pilgrim Writers, where we provide space, permission, encouragement, and instruction for you to tell the stories you need to tell. First, and most importantly, for yourself. Then, if the spirit moves, for your family and friends, or maybe even for the world.

"That was intense," more than one workshop participant has said to me over the years. I don't take it as a complaint, or an insult, because for me, intense is where the heart is. Life's too short for shallow. And although I don't want people to think every workshop leads to tears or wrestling with big questions, I do think you can tell your happy stories—your tales of accomplishment and pride—on your own. But you need community to birth and tend the hard stories. Being surrounded by others who are doing the same kind of excavation you're doing makes it a bit easier to keep the pen moving.

So, no. Not all Pilgrim Writers stories are sad. Not all of them are autobiographical. But I dare say the majority of them go beyond the surface.

It's the sharing of our stories that saves us.

That's what we're about when we gather together, be it in my home in Nashville or on the grounds of the Chautauqua Institution in New York, and various spots in-between. Churches, bookstores, retreat centers, private homes. Tennessee, Georgia, Florida, Mississippi, North Carolina. The locale doesn't matter. It's the connection that counts: between you and the words, and you and your fellow pilgrims.

When I first started offering workshops, back in 2007, I had no idea where it would lead, just that I had to try it. By that time I had met Pat Schneider, founder of Amherst Writers and Artists, and spent time at the Earlham School of Religion, a Quaker seminary in Indiana. Pat spent most of her life encouraging writers of all skill levels, and Quakers consider writing a ministry. Both of those life-changing encounters compelled me to look at writing differently. Before, I had seen it as a skill, an art form, and maybe, in a good year, a way to make a living. After, I knew that writing could be about outreach and connection and inclusion and understanding.

Something about helping people tell their stories without judgment was about all I could say when asked, "Why are you doing this?" Today, I have another answer: "Because I have seen how it brings people closer to themselves, closer to one another, and often, closer to the Divine and the world at large."

Within these pages you'll find pieces from some of the original Pilgrim Writers, brave women who showed up more than ten years ago when I announced I wanted to "try this writing group thing" and have kept coming. You'll also hear from folks who are newer to Pilgrim Writers, including a handful of men who have written with us along the way. Many of these writings grew out of prompts offered in workshop. We are of varying ages, backgrounds, experiences, skills, and goals. We live in different parts of the country. What brings us together is that we're people with stories to share.

Thank you for taking the time to read through this anthology. I hope you might write with us sometime. We'd love to hear your stories.

AMY LYLES WILSON, M.A., M.T.S.
Founder, Pilgrim Writers

BROKEN AND HEALED

SHERRY VANCE ALLEN

I have come to know you.
Your withered soul, broken and healed,
Broken and healed,
Broken and healed.

I see your face as young.
I see your face as old.
Your hands are softened, not hardened by the years.

I see your smile, the corners turned down a bit
but with a tinge of laughter.
I see your eyes, your powerful, strong, all-seeing and
all-guiding eyes.
They have seen the world and have served it up to you
and to many.
They have told your story to those who would see into them,
take the time to do so.

I see your heart.
I feel your heart.
I feel it flowing in and off of you, in and out, out of others, in and
out of life.

It knows you.
It reveals you.
You can trust it and it can trust you.
I have come to know you now.
I have come to know you.

JENNY

SHERRY VANCE ALLEN

The automated doors led me to a long tiled hall, the smell of bleach and disinfectant heavy in the air. I saw, room by room, patients who were young and old, men and women, black and white. Families sat by their sides, tired worn faces, prayers still on their lips. As I walked the corridor toward Jenny's room, the stench of vomit and urine and emptied bowels irritated my nose, and I felt guilty for thinking that.

I hurried to the nurses' station, anxious for news before entering the room. The worse cases were on this hall and there were few people who believed they would ever leave, but I was one of them who held hope. I just knew I would have Jenny back with me soon in her flannel pajamas, little feet walking over the hardwood floors, then running to hide behind the well-worn lace curtains in the kitchen, dragging around that curly-headed doll, shoes dangling from its feet.

All these images ran through my mind as I approached the desk. I had a half smile as I played this back in my head. Everything seemed so quiet at that moment, except for the backdrop of coughs and small cries. The head nurse approached me at the desk, charts in hand, white cotton suit and white rubber-soled shoes, an angel trying to save others from death.

She asked me to follow her. I inquired about Jenny's progress this morning since I had left. Did her fever break? I hoped the ice and wet cloths and alcohol bath had helped. Her breathing hadn't been as labored, and I think she smiled a little bit, too, but maybe I imagined that. Has the doctor been by yet? I wanted to talk to him about what to do next. Can we expect more of this or is there something else we need to consider? What do you think?

I kept asking all of these questions and she kept walking me down the corridor, leading me somewhere I had not been before. I followed along, anxious to hold Jenny's sweet little hands.

The nurse ushered me into a dimly lit room. I was confused at first, until I looked around and saw stained glass and two small candles burning. Father Dixon stood, with his arms open. I dropped to my knees.

SIKESTON, MISSOURI—1942

LINDA BARNICKEL

The little girl in Sikeston, Missouri: pigtails, boots.

The odor of flame and hot metal and charred flesh lingered with her, sunk in to her plaid coat that was a hand-me-down from her older sister, which she'd pass along to her baby sister in two more years. It always smelled like smoke.

No wonder she was the one who always crossed over to the other side of the street, any time she saw a black man coming. (It was supposed to be the other way around.)

Her momma told her: "Fear this."

Not the burning. Not the hatred. Not watching her daddy tend the fire or pulling on the rope. No, fear this. Fear this man. This man whom you do not know, whom you've never seen before. This man who has a child at home, just a little younger than you. This man who dared to look up from the ground, meet a white man's eyes in their passing on the street.

She was only seven. Taught to be afraid of this one man, and his daring, startling eyes—and the threat that posed, even from a distance—more than the hundreds of people who gathered to put him in his place, to teach him a lesson. Her father, cigarette dangling, looked away for a moment. She looked on.

Maybe she could never trust her father again, after that. She didn't understand what had happened to her town. Why her older brother, like her father, smiled for the camera, perverse pride on his face and in his hand. He kept a piece of the rope.

What would she tell her kids?

This is why the woman in the nursing home cries and strikes out when a black man comes to change her bed. Innocent bystander, seven years old, with eighty years of guilt.

VETERAN'S DAY

TOM CAMPBELL

As I look at my calendar before my next patient, I feel a twinge of irony. Joe, a decorated Vietnam veteran, will be my last appointment today, Veteran's Day. The time change has made his scheduled appointment time fall after dark. Darkness tends to evoke the memories, hovering about the edge of my awareness.

I have listened to veterans for many years. As I anticipate my session with Joe, I remember my first encounter with the trauma of war. In 1969, I was a medical intern, on call in a V.A. hospital. It was a slow night, dark and stormy. About midnight, a young man came in complaining of breathing difficulties.

"It's just nerves, Doc," he said. "I just got back from 'Nam and I can't get it out of my mind."

He said he was the only survivor of his patrol caught in the open while wading through a rice paddy, raked by automatic weapons fire. He survived by playing dead, trying to remain motionless while floating on his back with a through-and-through gunshot wound to his thigh. The pain was almost unbearable. With a mixture of terror and pain, his face bumping against floating human feces, he held out 'til dark. Hearing the soft crackle of small twigs in some nearby brush, he knew it was a human footstep. Unable to endure it anymore, he rolled the dice and whispered loudly, "GI?"

"Gyrine" [slang for Marine], came the reply. He was saved.

After the thirty to forty minutes it took to tell the story, he got up, shook my hand, and said, "Thanks for listening, Doc," and disappeared again into the night. I never saw him again and do not remember his name, but I have never forgotten his story or how the blackness of the night blurred with my emotions.

Joe, a short, stocky man with white hair, still curly but thinning, sits across from me now for his monthly appointment. As a retired V.A. mental health professional, he cannot afford to come more often. I have seen him for several years. His depression is now controlled by meds and his alcoholism finally subdued with AA and a good sponsor. We have bonded a bit around both being veterans, though

I have always been reluctant to claim my three years as a physician in Europe while all sorts of hell consumed other young men in Southeast Asia.

Today Joe is upset. His distress began with an email from someone in his old unit asking him to support upgrading their commander's Distinguished Service Cross to a Medal of Honor for his contribution during a battle. Joe Googled the battle, trying to remember some names, and ran across a reference to some previously lost television footage. Watching it, he was overcome with the old feelings of terror and rage, as alive and real as in the first moment of a young soldier's life. He was almost certain he'd seen himself, but he couldn't be sure. He did see the smoldering remains of his half-track military vehicle. He remembered the dead bodies in the bulldozed mass grave shown in the tape, and described the macabre searching for the bodies of the enemy after the battle.

"I've never told anyone this," he says. "One of the last ones, two or three days later, was in a ravine, bloated and swollen. I got a piece of communication wire around his shoulder at the armpit. But when I pulled, the arm came off like a baked chicken leg. I can never forget that smell. I was retching the whole time."

"There is no worse smell than that," I say.

"Worse than the firefight two nights before," he adds. "I was behind the bunker when the RPG exploded against the half-track and knocked me down. All I had was that damned first generation M-16 jamming every other round."

"Before they coated the works?"

"Fucking Lady Bird Johnson owned fifty-five percent of Colt Firearms," says Joe. "We had this rubber tube along the barrel to use to eject the spent cartridge. I said to the lieutenant, 'I don't have a weapon!' He told me to start carrying the wounded back to the aid station. I did that the rest of the night. That morning I was leaning against the bunker. I was exhausted, and my clothes were soaked with blood. I didn't give a damn about anything. Westmoreland and two one-stars came through. He said something about us not looking very military. Then one of the generals said, 'Good job, son.' It was just surreal."

Joe pauses for a bit. "I've got to go home from here. My son, his wife, and my wife are going to have a cake for Veteran's Day. 'Thank you for your service,' as they say now. They don't understand. I got drunk the night after seeing the video, but it didn't help. I just can't do that anymore. Truth is I'd kill myself if it wouldn't hurt my family. The anger still wells up in me white-hot. Something was taken from me and I've never gotten it back. I've never been the man I was."

"You mean the boy in you was lost?" I ask. "Something like your innocence and ability to feel safe again?"

He ponders a moment and says, "Yes, something like that. You try to tell family about it and they don't understand. Then you just give up."

As we speak, I am abruptly aware of being flooded with my own, milder flashbacks to the veteran's group I started in 1974 as a resident in psychiatry. There was a kid in the group who was a tunnel rat, shooting up with heroin to get the courage to crawl into the Viet Cong tunnels. I can still see him standing against the wall, shaking all over, as he tells the group about dragging his best buddy's body around for hours after a firefight until he could get out. Later he discovered he'd been dragging merely the torso, all that remained of his friend.

Images of my own exposure to death and dying come to mind. The failed codes, the desperate hope in the eyes of dying patients. I remember the eleven-year-old girl hit by a car and brought into the ER to be pronounced dead. I found a pulse, and we resuscitated her only to have her die in surgery. The bitterness of the loss, and the terror of realizing my responsibility for choices that could mean life and death for someone, began to haunt me. I remember my hospital commander begging me to treat his small embolic stroke there at our tiny hospital and not send him to the main referral hospital so he might avoid being medically boarded out of the Air Force. The anguish of choices that please no one yet affect lives in monumental ways.

I say to Joe, "You know I can understand death and dying and bodies and the burden of responsibilities that can cost people their lives, but I don't really understand what it feels like to have someone trying to kill you and what that does to you."

Joe responds, "That other action I told you about, the ambush where they were shooting at me from the trees and the dirt from the rounds was blowing into my eyes and mouth, it was so personal and so hopeless. That was when I had my first dissociative experience. I was outside and above my body looking down. I lost something over there, some vital part of me, and it has never come back."

"I had an anthropology professor once," I say. "His ship was sunk in a naval engagement, Guadalcanal or someplace like that. He was trying to climb into a life raft, as a Japanese sailor was trying to climb in from the other side. He shot him with his sidearm, blew his brains out with the .45. He talked about how it haunted him. Who was this man? Why did he have to kill him? What did it mean? He went into anthropology to try to make sense of the senselessness of what he had done."

Joe thinks for a moment. "Yeah, probably why I went to graduate school, too. Freed from the service, the great parties, met my wife. It just made sense. I worked all those years in the V.A. I guess I was trying to help myself as much as I was helping them. You'd think the V.A. would have kept me around, with my PTSD and Silver Star, but my anger kept getting me in trouble. Shit like claiming smoking cessation talks lasting ten minutes counted as therapy. Fuck 'em! I did what I had to do. I can live with that at least."

After a long pause, he says, "Well, thanks. I'm feeling better. Maybe I can manage the party now."

After making his next appointment, he stands to leave. Then he stops, turns around abruptly, and for the first time he spontaneously shakes my hand. As the door closes, my mind flashes to the grateful handshake of the veteran from long ago. At the same time, a haunting image floats across my mind. I see a young man, an amputee with the sore on his leg stump cleaned and dressed, putting on his prosthetic leg and walking away. His missing part is now covered up, all but invisible from the outside. I may have helped him adjust his mental defenses a little, but the loss endures as he, like the others, disappears again into the night.

HOW WILL I KNOW?

JULIE CANTRELL

How will I know when it is time? Time to end, time to start, time
to throw in the towel, or time to get on with it? What would such
awareness mean for me? To find out, I start today. Maybe this is the
beginning of the end, or maybe it is just what I need.

How will I spend my day? Helping people. I go to the shelter so
I can know the people there. Not merely what brought them off the
streets on this particular night, but really know them. I start with
the man in the corner, who looks like a lot of folks of advanced age.
Flowing silvery hair. Stubble on his weathered face. He is resting.
His clothes are clean. Well worn, yes, but something about his
appearance matters to him.

What joys has he known? Maybe he was married to the love of
his life; maybe they had a family and planned to grow old together.
Maybe the birth of a grandchild brought him joy.

What sorrows? Maybe the state of the world that grandchild was
born into gave him pause. Maybe he lost loved ones. I want to know
his joys and his sorrows, to honor them.

We assume we know. And therein lies the rub. We know only that
surely tears have flowed, because we see the crevices in his face. Could
they have been tears of joy? They make me think of the Grand Canyon,
which is often photographed to record a special moment in time. An
arid climate, but full of life from the river below. Ever changing, ever
permanent. I want to take a mental snapshot of the true beauty of the
man's face, like the old Polaroids, to preserve it for all time. Instant and
yet forever. I want to record the beauty of what has been.

I decide it is a beautiful canyon etched into that storied face. The
furrows show forth with the colors of the sun as it goes down into the
horizon. Glowing red, just the right amount, and hues of gold and copper.

Evidence of a long life, with its inherent moments of sadness and
joy. No beginning. No end. Circling round and round the path, until
they come back to their starting point, to do it all over again the next
day. Whatever stories they were to bring to him, yet another chapter
in his journey.

NEVER FORGET PULSE

STEPHANIE CENEDELLA

My dad taught me never to forget devastating tragedies; a common example was the Holocaust. He made a point to say, "If we forget about it we might allow something like it to happen again." But tragedies are painful and difficult to dredge up. An anniversary I imagine many want to forget is the 2016 shooting at the Pulse nightclub in Orlando that robbed forty-nine victims of their lives.

On the one-year anniversary I fought the responsibility my father had often charged to me. I dreaded reviewing the pain I had felt the previous summer when it happened. I struggled to navigate my way through the viciousness of what transpired that night in Orlando, and the aftermath of how I had felt connected to those lives lost. I didn't want to break open old wounds or remember how my heart felt shredded. How I, too, felt a victim through association. Because I had a sense of duty to my father, to our communities, I did what I knew I needed to. That afternoon I dug through a closet and resurrected a journal that housed raw feelings I'd written days after the event.

With trembling hands and pounding heart, I opened to the pages where I had rushed to dictate my tearful thoughts. I recognized all too well the fiercely scribbled, black-inked sentences that encompassed my personal grief. I'd scribed what I couldn't verbalize in hopes I could somehow move stuck, wretched feelings, and maybe even push them through me. Three days after the shooting I was beyond capacity with grief, and tried to make sense of my unrest. I remember well hoping the practical process of writing it all down would help shift the intensity of the moment beyond me.

> *June 15, 2016: This Orlando shooting has got me completely off kilter. Yes the news was shocking, that is to say, the entire act of killing those innocent gay people along with a few of their family members. The episode is rooted in bigotry though pockets of our society have chosen to believe living a gay life is no longer a problem. My family and I are familiar with bigotry. For me it has been a version of a boogieman I have been keenly aware of,*

watching over my shoulder for most of my life. I am sensitive to
these prejudices because my father was gay.

When the story broke I felt the incident come alive in every square inch of my body. I couldn't avoid it. Even as I turned away from details of the news, feelings were embroiled in my inner being. This tragedy is now added to all the other ugly historic headlines of gays being marginalized, denigrated, chastised, and brutally mistreated.

In my mind I recycled what happened. I visualized the dead, the terrified individuals who trembled as they begged for their lives to be spared. Secretly I always feared this kind of thing would happen. It is a constant pulse that throbs in my head and beats next to my heart. I'm *that* familiar with the intense negativity that people can feel toward gays. This is what comes with fearing for the safety of a loved one.

As news exploded on network television and throughout social media, I couldn't help but consider that this could have happened to my dad at any point in his life. A gay man from the mid-sixties on into contemporary times, he oftentimes walked what society looked at as a dark path. Up until his death a few years ago, I understood the life he lived was also one that was far from free. He was careful not to show he had a softer side. He often found the need to wear masks, even front a tough-guy exterior.

Growing up I learned to follow his lead. At times I, too, slipped on masks, and was careful not to reveal my father's true identity for concern my peers would sneer at the thought of a gay dad. I feared they might secretly make fun of him.

After decades of riding a closeted wave, dodging pockets of society's judgment, I finally began to open up. In my forties I started sharing my family profile, but only when I felt it was safe. In turn, I surfed the Internet and stumbled on a group of soul mates, a handful of female adults who had a similar understanding of the slippery slope connected to a gay dad. They, too, had lived frustrated lives working to fit a gay father into society, finding it challenging to defend negativity from those who disagreed with a father's sexuality.

I found a home with these sisters who had been on a common journey to find place and family. Through them I came to believe that the LGBT family is also a part of my family. Because my father was a gay man I understood how and why it was important to find community and the need to seek shelter. Pulse was just that kind of place. It held many purposes for many people.

From a distance, the nightclub patrons were my people. The onset of the mass shooting, now a mass tragedy, has caused me to place deeper meaning on why the people at Pulse wanted to dance. I believe they did so to release and create joy. They found Pulse to be a safe space, a place to feel free.

As of January 2016, I, too, begin to dance. I do so religiously in a local studio two days a week. In six short months I clock many exhilarating sessions that allow me a much-needed sense of freedom.

When I attend my first class after the shooting, in addition to the immense pool of shock and loss, I am devastated as I think about how this has forced my teenage children to confront such aggressive bigotry. Yet I'm also struck by the network of connection. That when horrific acts like the one at Pulse take place, I realize we are more connected than we think. My teens' grandfather was a gay man. Surely now they realize that he could have been killed simply for being gay. They must also understand, in a new and alarming way, that hatred is powerfully strong. That intolerance is still alive. My mind races as I realize I need my dance class to serve as an exorcism.

I am distraught as I enter the dance studio. Julia, my instructor, takes a few moments at the onset of class to set intention. Today we will dance for those who no longer can. We will also try to work through the angst this recent tragedy has brought us on a personal level, hoping to move through how and why it happened.

Although I struggle to find my footing at first, I'm thankful for feeling less rigid by the end of the third song. My limbs begin to sync with the music. What a gift it is to dance freely. Soon thereafter I feel the beginning of a much-needed lift of weight—the enormous built-up heft of the past days' news. The sadness has begun to loosen its tight grip.

Thirty minutes into the rhythmic movements, my body continues to open to the pulses of music. Barefooted, I slam my feet onto the dance floor, gliding my body through the air on beat. More confident with my motions, I return to thinking of the innocent gay people in the club, their bereaved friends, and their families. I feel a kinship to my LGBT community. In this moment of dance it also occurs to me that the victims' ability to dance was taken away, as was their ability to express themselves freely. Lost in thought I lose my footing. I begin to fume. I can't stand the unfairness of it all. My sensitive soul caves and aches. I realize that due to the extent at which I am affected by the lost lives I, too, am paying for the act of bigotry. I suddenly feel a sense of responsibility.

Because I *can*, I *need* to keep dancing. Though my eyes gloss over with tears I pick up my pace. I try with all my might to focus, stay in step with the other dancers, all the while trying to work through the mass of thoughts and feelings. I *will* myself to keep up.

After forty-five minutes of an aggressive whirlwind, flinging myself about the balmy studio, I note a newfound sense of solace. I'm exhausted. I've shed all that I'd held in and am closer to calm than I've been since I'd heard the news. For that I am grateful.

I rest hands on hips and catch my breath while Julia moves to the edge of the room to dim the lights, signaling the start of our cool down. Again with purposeful intention, she selects the words of John Lennon's song "Imagine" to guide us into a peaceful resting place. Following her lead, I bend to stretch my right leg. With a slight bounce I dip my head to go even deeper, a bit closer to the floor. Without warning I feel a wall of tears rain down.

I brush tears across my cheeks and think, *Oh how I long for that place, that time when all people will live in harmony.* My insides clutch as I wish for brighter days. Then I turn to stretch to the other side. I pray, *Someday soon may we all simultaneously find that place.*

During each cool down Julia tells us when to switch sides or change poses. Today she honors the space with silence, so we shadow her long, lean body movements. Still crying, I'm aware I am unraveling. I dart my eyes at others, embarrassed. On the outside at least, they don't appear to share my history. Maybe their brains—and bodies—haven't recorded historical gay tragedies in the same way.

I worry my emotions might not subside. That is, until the soundtrack transitions from Lennon to Louis Armstrong's "What A Wonderful World." The song is less somber and more uplifting. The words are bright and colorful. They ring softly, and somehow flow through our outstretched dancer bodies.

The soothing tone brings a wind of change to my internal hurt. I realize that instead of wallowing in sorrow, I can pray for hope. In a moment, I decide that's just it. It can be that simple. We live in a wonderful world with all kinds of wonderful people. If we could all see that—if we could all lead our children to see that, our world could be a wonderful, safe place.

I shift significantly. I am still fragile, but hopeful. Class ends and the other dancers step out quietly while I sit, working to process where today's dance has taken me, and try to gather myself. Julia moves toward me, towering over my five-foot frame. She sits down next to me, and engulfs me in her arms. As she cradles me, we begin to weep. After several minutes she whispers, "Keep playing music and just keep dancing."

Julia is a safe house who holds my story. She knows I carry within me a lifetime of worry surrounding a longing for others to accept my father for who he was. After a few minutes, I work to pull myself together. I am grateful for her love and understand there is no need to tell her as much. She knows. I nod a thank-you and smile for the beautiful ritual of dance she has afforded me. Then I stand to walk down the narrow hallway and out into the mid-morning sunshine toward my car. I vow—for my sake and for those who can no longer do so—to keep dancing. I try to believe that someday soon, people can and will live as one in our wonderful world.

A few short weeks later my daughter attended a theater camp where more than 200 campers created a video remake of Jackie Shannon's 1965 hit, "What the World Needs Now." The campers came together to respond to a challenge from Broadway for Orlando, the charitable initiative founded by Broadway Records to support victims of the Pulse shooting. The organization's YouTube video was a call to action and a means to tap into the hearts of those around the world.

Determined to make some noise of their own, the campers' teenage voices rang out as a new generation sending a hopeful message. I dreamed it would cause a ripple effect to manifest change in the world. Tens of thousands viewed the recording and forwarded it through social media. I listened to their angelic voices many times over, and was moved each time. I consider it a prayer for loving, positive change. For people to stop, take a breath, and consider how significant the moment was and how necessary it is to create real change. My heart hoped our world was ready for this. My head remained skeptical.

A year after the Pulse tragedy, I realize my dad was absolutely right. We need to keep talking. Change is still needed. Minds still need convincing. People still need to be granted respect for who they are and whom they chose to love. We need to teach our children to be stewards of change. We need to do so until we solve *why* hate crimes continue to take place. Because yet another mass shooting occurred on February 14, 2018, at Marjory Stoneman Douglas High School in Florida, where seventeen more innocent lives were taken. The hate and intolerance have gone on too long. Until we get it right it, until our world understands, truly feels the gravity of the repercussions, injustice toward gays will keep happening. Until the lessons are learned.

The forty-nine people who lost their lives at the Pulse nightclub were more than victims: they were strong survivors, searching for what everyone wants, what I want for my children in this lifetime. What my father wanted. Respect. Acceptance.

THE FOREST

LISA DAMMERT

Only the forest knows my pain,
the rot and decay.
Water flowing over rocks
slicing them apart molecule by molecule
like time strips away life
breath by breath.
Only the forest knows,
how change can ravage
and heal.
Old gives way to new.
Every season, brutal in its own right
yields in the end.

ANGELS IN THE CLOUDS

CECE DUBOIS

When I was a child, I could see angels in the clouds. The day I ran away from school, after the woman at the gas station took me home, I lay on my bed and watched them out the window. That was the day my daddy dropped me off at kindergarten late again. The day Sister Isabel said latecomers would get in serious trouble.

I waited till Daddy had driven his car out of the school parking lot. Then, instead of pulling open the heavy door and going inside, I turned around and walked away.

I walked my five-year-old self across the busy intersection in rush-hour traffic. I walked as far as the culvert leading down to the river. The one the bridge crossed over, the one where every time Daddy drove across my brother sat on the floorboard in the back seat and squeezed his eyes closed. That one. I sat in the tall grass, and thought to myself: Where should I go now? I'm stuck. A little thread of panic made my heart jump, and for a minute I thought I might cry.

I looked over my shoulder at the Phillips 66 station on the corner. There were people there, so I got up and made my way toward them. My legs were itchy from the grass, and I was getting sweaty. I tried to unbutton my coat, but I couldn't make my fingers work right.

I stepped onto the concrete and saw a lady with a little girl sitting in their car. The filling station guy was checking her oil. I wasn't supposed to talk to strangers, but I thought a little girl's mama might be okay.

I wandered closer, stopped a little ways from the car, and stared. The woman was paying the gas station man when she saw me. She sat there for a minute, and then she and her little girl got out of the car and came over to me.

"Honey, where's your mama?" she said.

"At home," I whispered.

"Do you know your address?"

"22336."

"I don't think that's an address. Is that your phone number?"

I was confused. I knew it was something, I just wasn't sure what. I dropped my head, looked up at her under my eyelashes, and sucked my finger.

She must have decided she couldn't leave me there, so she put me in the car with her little girl. I remember thinking she smelled like flowers. Her little girl had curly hair and dimples. Her bonnet matched her coat.

The lady gave us each a stick of Wrigley's Spearmint, and when we got to her house she called my mother at 22336. She wrote down my address, then she and her little girl carried me home.

When we got there my mother thanked the woman profusely, but once the door was closed behind them, she was furious. We were Catholics, and that woman was the wife of a Protestant preacher. How could I have embarrassed her like that? She frowned, held her hand under my chin, and made me spit out my gum.

It was Mama's laundry day. She stripped off my clothes down to my undershirt, panties, and socks. She told me to go get on my bed and stay there. The sheets were being washed, so I laid down on the mattress pad and scooched over to look out the window. That's when I saw them. The angels. I'd seen them before. But that day, more than ever, I was glad they were there. And given the adventure I'd just been through, it seemed pretty clear they'd been with me all along.

MAYBE

CECE DUBOIS

Things in my life are the way they are, based on every choice I've made. They laid a road, end to end, that brought me here to this table today. Good or bad, for better or worse, here I sit; my greasy hair under a ball cap, my thoughts scattered, and the censor in my brain telling me that what I'm writing now is not worth a damn.

I get sick of hearing my own voice tell my own stories. Are other people as sick of it as I am? I don't want to write cute, or clever. As Hemingway says, write real, about what hurts. I've kerfed around the edges of the pain for years, never hitting it dead center. I guess that's real if you're digging a trench, but I'm sort of stuck down here, looking for truth. And trying to dig my way out.

I could write about birds. But then my brain goes to the parakeet we had at 1135 South Quaker. My mother named it Perry Como. He was blue, with black wing tips, and a spot of lime green between his eyes. Thinking of him now I can smell his birdseed and that cage with the newspapers in the bottom.

When they let Perry out of that cage, he flew up and sat on the curtain rods. Every time he flew his wings made a loud flapping sound that scared my little brother.

Sometimes my mother would open Perry's cage door, and wait. When my brother came walking through the living room, suddenly Perry would swoop down. My brother would scream and dive under the table, clutching the legs and sobbing. My mother raised her eyebrows, took a drag off her cigarette, and laughed. That taught me some pretty twisted things about how people treat those they claim to love. So yeah … count that little nugget as a lob to the center of the pain from the trenches.

Or maybe I could write about being a teenager. And dating.

Maybe I could write about the night a boy came to pick me up, and he had a long fringe of bangs. My little sisters peeked around the door, giggling, "It's a Beatle!" My dad growled, "Is that your hair, boy, or is that a wig?"

Or I could write about another time my date arrived to take me to the school dance. He drove his car, parked, and my father drove us to school in our '51 two-door Pontiac. The two-door thing is relevant because Dad and my date sat in the front, and I climbed into the back. In my formal. The thing I'll never forget is the glowing orange hood ornament. I locked my eyes on Chief Pontiac all the way to school, trying to ignore the awkward silence.

Maybe I could write about the faith, and the sense of humor, that have carried me on angel wings through the darkest of days, the brokenest of hearts. How, even in those moments…my date with the Beatles hair, me sitting in the back seat of that car…even then, in the recesses of my mind, I knew: "This is the rich stuff of which stories are made. I will write about this one day."

Maybe today, sitting here at this table, wearing my ball cap, is that time.

HUMMINGBIRD ANGELS

SUSAN SPEAR DYER

The angels hover over the lifeless body of the young man. Darting carefully above, back and forth, in and out like hummingbirds collecting nectar from a beautiful flower. Each busy taking care of its work, to guard this heart while it hemorrhages. All working in tandem, knowing just what to do. They are hummingbird angels with soft faces and delicate feathery wings. They create an invisible tent of love, safety, and compassion for this young man as he lies in a fetal position on the ground. Does he know they are present to help him slip by his threshold guardians? He cannot see them because his eyelids are closed. He cannot know. But she does.

His mother watches from the hilltop. She hasn't believed in angels—until now. She sees her son lying lifeless and can do nothing. She knows this is his initiation into manhood and if he gets up, he must walk on alone, his wound inflicted by angry, hateful words from a bitter father revealing the Truth of a broken family.

She has shielded the son from this Truth for twenty years. Watching her child suffer, unable to help, is her worst nightmare. Her heart is sliced open and hemorrhages, too, as she watches him slip into a place of death. The mother knows she can do nothing to recover his innocence.

He is a bright, happy, and gifted son, sensitive and creative, the light of her life. She thinks he is a gift from the Universe. As she watches silently, he does not stir. But the hummingbird angels keep their steady vigil. She is amazed at their presence and the comfort they bring to her, even in her despair. She feels no need to speak to them or to tell them what to do, knowing that her role is only as an observer now. She will watch and wait, silently, and pray, and try again to forgive. Because her son's heart is more important than continued battles for power. She wonders how long it will take for his eyes to open, for she knows they will. She has felt the same sharp arrow to her heart, inflicted by the same hands trembling with bitterness.

He will sit up and walk, he will be reborn, because he is strong and he has the hummingbird angels to light his path. Does he know this wounding is his first rite of passage at the beginning of his life's journey? He will learn to fly on his own, and she trusts his path will be as sacred as the chances he takes to share his light and his love. And so, she is content to keep her faithful vigil.

Amen

NURSE RHONDA

KAREN FENTRESS

It all started before I ever met her. She is who I planned to avoid. But, Momma got sick, and Daddy hates waiting. So there I am, at work, flummoxed by my own errors, when I get the text I hate to see. The one from Sister that says, *Call me, asap.* So I do, finally.

But I've been in a too-long meeting. When I see the words formed from tiny pixels, I have a more than a tiny panic. Sister, far away and sounding as if she is in a deep well of her own, asks that question I hate to hear: "Have you talked to Dad?"

"Well, yes, after lunch," is my almost hopeless reply.

"Then I guess you know Mom is at the hospital."

And, I don't have to tell you what she said is a spear to my weary, unarmed mind. Because at this point, I don't know Nurse Rhonda yet, and I don't want to have to.

It's almost 4:30 in the afternoon in my town, my sister is coasting away from me, down the interstate, telling me Momma is at the ER. And these damned stacks of paper in this godforsaken office stare me down, saying, *Are you listening—are you going to pray now—are you really going to waste your time?*

But I do, I give the impotent stacks of paper the finger, turn my back on their confusing speech, and cry out to the only God who lets me pray and doesn't rub me out for my unbelief.

Before I can summon the mettle to call my daddy, I have to weep a little.

So I do, and I wipe the snot off my nose when I leave the bathroom stall. I phone him and he answers in his bewildered, eighty-two-year-old voice.

"Yeah. Karen. We're here. Are you coming? Will you feed Sam? You don't need to come. We are all right. Go feed Sam. Watch some basketball. We'll be home later. We are getting some tests. Yes. I don't know what it is. They think it could be a clot. It's that place on her leg. Well, come if you want to. Okay. We are all right."

Jesus. Jesus. I say. He is so old.

At this point, I think surely an hour has passed, but when I look at the time, it's only 4:40. And Rhonda, the nurse, is still out there, holding it together 'til all hell breaks loose. This is the part of the story where your narrator realizes she can't do this doubting on her own.

So I text the merry band of friends who can barely lift their heads either, but they do. And oh. They do. But we know it is not they who *do* a thing. It is beyond my finitude to tell you, but this God to whom we cry longs for us to come. So we do. Over and over. And, again. And He, being who He is, supplies what we, the wounded, sick, and sore, need to approach. Ad infinitum.

It's an hour before Rhonda's shift starts. I still don't know this boisterous charge nurse. My effort to pay attention at work until I can take it no more lasts until about 6:00. After the sweet believing prayers of friends, I do every vain thing I can in my own power to quell the fear. Fruitless. Fruitless. On the way to the hospital, I daydream about Momma. Beginnings. Endings. I'm foggy and tired.

I paste a sunny face on my cloudy one and walk into the crowded ER of a major trauma hospital, on a Friday, for Pete's sake. Though I could not see her, a tall hefty woman breezes through the employee alcove, and begins her night of rescue. Her name is Rhonda, which means "good spear": rhon=spear; da=good.

I'm barely seated in the waiting room when the lady's voice on the intercom calls *Juaneeeta. Feeentriss....*

Daddy rolls his eyes, gathers his sports page, obits, op-ed pages, wool cap, ratty sweater, leather jacket, and begins the foot race to the room. Following the man whose six-foot stride she loves with an undying heart is my hobbling mother, who, though she is recovering from hip surgery, moves with purpose to see this difficulty to its conclusion. I'm astonished she believes the hard times are possible. She has had lots of practice.

I lag behind in awe, and stare as they follow a man with a clipboard. I almost lose them—I'm distracted by the maze of ER rooms peopled with the sick and all the beeping sounds—but the shock of Daddy's silver, mussed hair catches my attention. He stands tall and stooped in his faded corduroy trousers, cardigan sweater, and Merrell walking shoes, gripping his aforementioned worldly possessions. By the time I catch up, Momma is already perched on the exam bed. In her worst hour, she shines. Is that why she's here, to teach us how to reflect the sun?

Momma is sick, and Daddy hates waiting.

I think I said that before, but dear Jesus, does it bear repeating. It is nearly 6:45 p.m.; this is about the time it occurs to my poor daddy that he is trapped.

"We've been here since 4:00," he growls in a way that makes me love him more. His face is full of consternation, worry, doubt, and a touch of indignation. The rant escalates, ever slow: "The physical therapist thinks it's a clot, that's why we're stuck in this mess." I look at Momma. Her face is a polished stone. The day shift nurse, I forget her name, a skinny predecessor to Nurse Rhonda, comes in, impersonating a waif. Ivory skin lies on her timid white bones. One question from Daddy and she wilts. Off-put, and afraid, they each dance a brittle jig. She leaves after perfunctory nurse duties of making sure Momma is Momma and asks, for what Momma says is the seventh time, the same questions she answered already, six times, I guess. I notice, as the nameless nurse departs by way of the curtained boundary, that she too, is adorned in a cardigan sweater.

It is the shift change, and it is my Daddy's otherworldly wisdom about his lack of patience that saves lives. As he walks out, he pecks his sweet wife on the cheek, wondering aloud if she believes he is abandoning her. Screwing her relief and courage to the sticking place, she offers more grace than he deserves.

"No, Charles. Go home, get some rest."

"I love you, Juanita."

"I love you, too, Charles."

I want to sob, but I hide in the river. Daddy's form fades out the door when in walks a stout, mullet-wearing, deliverer clad in blue scrubs. She barks instructions to her night-shift partner, a boyish nurse whose name is Joshua. Yes, the Bible name. I hope you don't miss that.

This is the place in the tale where I ache for the real presence of my honest-to-god superhero sister. Right this second, I'm not in Egypt in the desert. Since she might as well be a world away, that metaphor will not suffice. I'm on the face of a peak in the Himalayas. She is a Nepalese trail guide. By the way, she does wear funny hats. I know how inept a thinker I am when the stress of the climbing rope is taut and I don't know which foot to move next. Then, Momma smiles at me, and I see our Nepalese guide in her burning eyes. I text my sister to say Daddy went home, and that's when our protagonist introduces herself to Momma. It is 7:15.

"Hello, my name is Rhonda, and I'll be your nurse."

I knew then she would carry us across the Red Sea on her back if she had to. I wish you could see her. The grace of the one who sent her compels me to dream she is a curious amalgam of many friends and relations. An antique oddity of a different time, she is puffy overweight, a smoker, and probably belts whiskey with the boys. She perspires like a whore in church, and is not a picture of health. But who is, really? She moves like a momma bear, stealthy and cunning. She is old school, and would probably wrestle you to the ground and kick your whiny ass if you crossed her in the pool hall.

My phone battery dies as the night wanes into the next day's wee hours. The connection to my navigator in the funny Nepalese hat is at risk, and I wonder what the blue-eyed sister would think of this Moses nurse. I know they might clash. Nurses nearly always do. But, for the sake of my sister, risking the intersection of mixed metaphor yet again, were they on a mountain in the Himalayas together with a crowd of infirm climbers, they'd both make sure the best and first rope was for the sick.

My sister asks at one point, "Are the nurses taking good care of her?" I assure her Rhonda has the good rope. Momma leaves the room for test after test. They are searching for a clot that ultimately isn't found; her blood runs mottled, but free of danger. Even so, it's eight hours before we know this. Rhonda mutters as she charts, attends to details like getting blankets, checks vitals, and pursues the ghosts who pose as doctors. There are blisters on her feet of deliverance.

I imagine the jangled nerves of my sister as the bracing wind of the high, faraway mountain assails her body and her soul. She longs to be near and every hour she's not here, she dies a little. She has tossed me the best rope and wills me to help Mother make the ascent.

Rhonda peeks in on Momma, checks her vitals, eyeballs the inflamed site, and suggests keeping her leg still and up is best. Momma complies. Rhonda pauses, laying a hand on the disheveled bed, and assures her it will not be long. She leaves by way of the horrid curtain, and it flaps in the stale air. A daughter's belief wavers.

Momma says, "She's a tough old bird, but she's got a kind heart." Unconvinced, I nod and get up to stretch my legs. The hall of the ER is scattered with the grimacing and sleeping; my hard heart wonders, who is faking? A resident physician articulates in a flat voice,"It will not be long now" and disappears. *Pfft*, I say. *How long, O Lord?*

Back in the room, it is 1:15 a.m., and Rhonda takes off her clogs. "These damn things keep makin' a blister on my toe," she declares, exasperated. Momma lies waiting in near perfect peace. I inquire what's become of the radiologist's report.

"This is ridiculous," says Rhonda. "I'm gonna find him myself."

After forty minutes and finally triumphant, our heroine waves discharge papers in time to save me from more grumbling. I fetch Momma's shoes. Dry as a bone and travel weary, we climb to the other side of the water. A gulf of crashing spray separates us from the valiant advocate I never wanted to know.

Now free, I look across the water to see Rhonda wiping the brow of a feverish traveler. Cool night air bathes my face as the sliding door of the ER opens. Watching her every step, I follow my limping momma to the Promised Land.

FURY

KAREN FENTRESS

It has been said, "If you are not outraged, you are not paying attention." Let me be clear. I've been staring at this abject evil so long my eyes are about to fall out of my head. I look away, though. I got my single malt. I got opera. I got the wailing verse of Bob Dylan and pristine sonnets of Richard Wilbur. I look away real good. Days are full of darkness. So you may ask, *How in hell can darkness ever be full?* I don't know, but you could ask the lady who's been beat in the head so many times by her lover she has a constant buzzing in one ear and can't hear much out of the other. Her eyesight is damn near gone. She's still living with this lover. Living and loving. Days are also full of loss. Purity and trust have dwindled like stale water down a corroded drain. Once bright-eyed boys and girls now see love as a snake in the night, slithering in their beds. Ruin creeps into homes, schools, and places built for worship. Nobody wants to hear this. Nobody. It is the sad tune in a forever minor key: violence, absence of peace, and the presence of fear. My question is this: Would we even know how to respond if there weren't an "other" to whom we could rail and weep? Would we recognize the dark if there weren't some beacon, some standard, some siren? To hell with positive thinking. Get your hands dirty. Help your frightened neighbor. Nurse the wounded. Scatter the darkness with the fury of light.

CHARLIE'S SONG

KAREN FENTRESS

Our story died like pitiful flat rocks
your daddy skipped on Sugartree Creek.
Our story died on the night of Christmas.
Christ's mass:
When God himself entered temporal time,
you up and went home.

Dear boy whom I barely met,
I'm banking your story goes on.
Your fair blond curls blow in the vast east wind,
Lit by the laughing moon.

Though our threads are untwined
in the here and now, on *that day,*
that day,
when I'm done calling to deep after deep;
when there will be no more not yet.
On *that* day, days will be forever.

Our story will begin again:
Looking for the hidden sea,
walking on shimmering streets,
clambering over jeweled gates.

Our story will be reborn;
and we will always be telling it.

WRITING GROUP

AMI FLETCHER

Go. Drive there. Even if you don't know why you're going.
Go. Drive there. Even if you don't know why you're going.
Pay attention to everything that's said and done.
Pay attention to everything that's said and done.
Write the check and get your money's worth.

Go happy and enjoy. Write miffed. Pay everything to Amy Lyles.
Don't drive there. Don't get your money's worth.

Write whatever Amy Lyles says to write.
Write whatever Amy Lyles says to write.
Don't get miffed by something somebody says.
Don't get miffed by something somebody says.
Enjoy the class and let it seep into you for the rest of the day.

Go happy and enjoy. Write miffed. Pay everything to Amy Lyles.
Don't drive there. Don't get your money's worth.

Be happy. Enjoy saying, "I'm glad I'm alive today."
Be happy. Enjoy saying, "I'm glad I'm alive today."
Feel gratitude well up inside.
Feel gratitude well up inside.
Be happy saying, "I'm alive today."

Go happy and enjoy. Write miffed. Pay everything to Amy Lyles.
Don't drive there. Don't get your money's worth.

LULLABY

MANDY FORD

"Mommy, will you rock me?" he says in the room lit by two
nightlights and insulated by artificial ocean sounds.
"You're too big to be rocked," is my immediate response.
A small whimper. The same request again. This time pleading.
I'm exhausted. Frustrated. Aching for a bit of time to call my own.
You just want to be rocked.
To feel the strong yet gentle hold my arms offer. The slow rocking as
your toes graze the carpet each time I bow to the right.
My right arm cradles your long lean legs, the crook of my elbow a
sling for your limp knees. You melt into me.
"What song do you want?" This plays on repeat most nights,
sometimes four or five times before your sleep comes.
"I love you Benny," you whisper. This is my made-up lullaby.
Back and forth our bodies sway in unison as I softly sing the words,
"I love you Benny, oh yes I do." It is a short session, much unlike
the ones when rocking was a part of our routine, in a proper chair,
the repetitive sway making my eyes as heavy as yours, both of us
drifting off to a quiet place together.
I often admire your feet. Still untouched by the world. Smooth skin.
No calluses or cracks. They remind me that your spirit is the same,
so naive to this world that my own grown-up heart aches.
You just want to be rocked.
And so we do.

"THAT'S MY GIRL"

MANDY FORD

"That's my girl," she says.
I don't know if it's the Southern accent
or the motherly inflection that does it for me.
I hold them in my mouth for a while,
my tongue absorbing their sweetness before I drink them down.
They sustain me, those three words.
They call up each of my insecurities, my fears, my scars,
and give them a tight squeeze around the neck;
then politely tell them where to go.

HOLD ME CLOSER, TINY DANCER

EVE HUTCHERSON

Scene: Spring dance recital.

Location: A clean, bright church in the heart of downtown Nashville.

Players: Scores of dance students in assorted matching ensembles, ranging from restless, over-stimulated three-year-olds in tremulous tutus to high-school students demurely draped and displaying the detached nonchalance of stage veterans.

Audience: Efficient young parents, speeding each dancer to the correct pre-show location and trailed by doting grandparents, aunts, uncles, and friends.

If you have ever attended a dance performance to witness the efforts of your own child or another apple of your eye, you will know the fundamental laws of such occasions that universally apply.

The first is that the length of the program will appall you. How many children in the average metro area can possibly be enrolled in tap, ballet, and modern dance? Thousands, apparently.

The second law is that while you may expend your best self to claim a good seat early, your child's number is not first. Or second. It is buried deep into the program, testing will and endurance, especially of the Tiny Dancers and those who love them most. And finally, consideration for the feelings of others must prevail. Take care about laughing audibly at someone else's child, because yours might do something even funnier.

Settling into the pew and enjoying the pre-show anticipation in the air, I joined our three-year-old Sis's paternal grandparents with warm appreciation for their effort to drive three hours to attend. A quick scan of the program prompted a deep, cleansing breath. The entertainment featured a series of twenty-two performances, and Sis and her ensemble were slotted at number seventeen. A cheerful, commanding female claimed the microphone to announce the requisites and signal for lights down and music up. We were off.

Well, one wants to do the right thing, of course, and clap appreciatively for all performances. Nevertheless, about the time that some ten Tinies in leotards of multi-colored sequins were wreaking their particular brand of havoc onstage, the mind began to wander. Memory hovered on the testimony of the immortal Bertie Wooster, hero and foil of the Jeeves stories of British humorist P. G. Wodehouse. Recalling a series of amateur performances at a village concert, Bertie described the opening violin solo like this:

"It was loud in spots, and less loud in other spots, and it had that quality I have noticed in all violin solos, which is seeming to last much longer than it actually did."

Jarred out of the Wodehouse analogy by the next enthusiastic round of applause from the commendably patient audience, I refocused and realized something interesting. By the time we clocked into about dance number eight or nine, patterns emerged. Without commentary on child psychology or related questions, I can vouch that each Tiny Troupe featured the following roles, whether undertaken voluntarily or not.

The Free Bird: Detaches self from group, ignores teacher and all other performers, runs wildly around the stage perimeter in some routine of the dancer's own devising. Some Free Birds have to be removed from the stage by force majeure at the conclusion of the number.

The Statue: Stands frozen in terror, staring fixedly into audience. Cannot move feet, may clutch hands, possibly in subconscious plea for removal. Bravely resists crying but clearly would like to.

The Two-Timer: Cannot decide whether to follow teacher or fellow performers so alternates, turning from front-facing to peer-view position and back again, remaining a few steps behind throughout. Our Sis takes this role and performs it with enthusiasm.

The Good Soldier: Stays in designated position, eyes locked on teacher, following carefully with intense concentration. Demonstrates total commitment, but may or may not look happy about it.

The Star That's Born: This performer follows the routine to perfection, even adding a flourish or two of his or her own, here and there. Lights up with genuine delight at the applause of the audience, floats off stage on a cloud.

Do these roles illuminate windows into the future for these Tinies, and into the paths they pursue? I would pay excellent money to reconvene them in about twenty years and find out, but I will have to settle for watching our Sis.

She seemed more interested in her sparkling outfit and post-performance flowers than the actual dance, and it occurred to me I would have felt the same in her tiny ballet shoes. Nevertheless, all survived and success was ultimately declared.

Meanwhile, the real heroes of the evening were the teachers, who led their Tiny Troupes through their routines with unwavering grace, all the while radiating encouragement. Proving that indeed the show must go on, they were neither distracted by the Free Birds nor derailed by the Two-Timers. Mentally I add teachers to my own private list of heroes, which includes firefighters, cops, plumbers, tech support specialists, and Seal Team Six. They have heard and seen it all, and life holds no further surprises for them. Had I encountered one of these teachers, one of these beacons of hope, when departing at the evening's conclusion, I would have been tempted to salute.

HANDING DOWN THE ANCESTRAL SEAT

EVE HUTCHERSON

A few years back I read a fascinating book about Te Maori, the first United States exhibition of ancient art from the native Maori people of New Zealand. Elaborate tribal rituals symbolizing honor for, and protection of, the ancestral artists, who are believed by the Maori to spiritually inhabit the art they created, preceded the opening of the exhibit at the Metropolitan Museum in New York.

The notion of beloved spirits inhabiting objects is easy for me to accept on a spiritual level. It also prompted me to extend the concept on a different plane toward my mother, who throughout her adult life has served as custodian and curator of a large collection of family treasures handed down through various branches of our family tree. As years passed and circumstances caused the collection to grow, my father teased her about her strong affection for these items, which range from jewelry and handbags to furniture, artwork, china, and the like. Ours is a blessed but certainly not wealthy family, so the value of the treasures spikes much higher on the emotional scale than on the financial. We are unlikely candidates for big surprises on *Antiques Roadshow*.

Whether my ancestors owned, or created, these treasures, it mesmerizes me to consider what their spirits, if residing therein, could pass on to us. Could I replicate the hospitality at my own dinner parties that always illuminated my parents' home by remembering to pull out my mother's crystal wine glasses? Could I someday achieve tournament-winning putting, like my grandfather, if I keep polishing his silver golf trophies, or will I just inherit his predilection for corny golf jokes? Can I emulate with my little family the long conversations I had with my dad if I take good care of the old maple rocking chair I sat in, across from his favorite perch in the den, when we chatted?

Many of these objects are lovely to behold and an honor to own. And then there are others, causing one to wonder where reason factors in. These varying views might be over style; sometimes for condition. Either was something we freely commented on when my generation was younger, when one is unerringly certain of so very many things. My mother generally accepted such opinions with her characteristic equanimity.

Nowadays, honesty compels me to admit that these illogical attachments to ancestral objects claim us eventually, as we move to a more reminiscent season of life. There's an ancient, dented tin measuring cup with a bent, cock-eyed handle tucked in my kitchen drawer that I can't relinquish, so it stays nestled there next to its shinier, more legible modern counterparts. For years my sister clung stubbornly to an old, thin aluminum spatula descended from we aren't sure where, swearing it was the only implement in her kitchen that could pry absolutely anything out of a skillet. Rust finally sent that one to the trashcan.

Carefully preserving treasures for children, too, my mother sent one of her favorites to my daughter after the birth of the first great-grandchild. This miniature, Windsor-shaped wicker rocking chair, freshly painted, was a gift to my mother from her own grandfather when she was a child, growing up in a small mountain town in eastern Kentucky eight decades ago. That makes the current occupants the fourth generation to rock baby dolls and bunnies in the tiny chair, which I long ago christened The Ancestral Seat. Will my mother's spirit in the little rocker impart her sense of humor, compassion, and common sense? If so, it would also surely convey a rather particular expectation that children should behave, help their family members, and take good care of older people.

My own favorite family treasure is a round, hardwood table with a rattan pedestal base, acquired by my parents in the Philippines nearly sixty years ago and shipped home to occupy their kitchen for the remainder of their married life. Growing up, we ate all family meals at this table, where my brother routinely knocked over his milk and my sister leaned back and fell over in her chair. Around its circumference occurred all kinds of family dialogue, more than a few pointedly delivered parental instructions, and equal parts smart-aleck teenage commentary. It bears cigarette burns and other scars from years of service at the center of a big, raucous family. When my mother moved to a smaller home not long ago, there was no spot for the old rattan warrior.

"I guess we'll get rid of it," said my sister, who patiently organized the sharing or disposal of items that had to find new homes.

"Not a chance," I said. Whether it lands on my porch for outdoor dinners, in the kitchen, or some space not yet imagined, the table, and whatever spirits it harbors, stays with me. With us.

EVIDENCE OF AUTUMN

JANIS LOVECCHIO

The fragrance of change is layered.
Subtle at first, carried on a breeze that hints at transition.
An initial crispness followed by the distinct fragrance of decay.
Sweet dyings and profound renderings alert
only those senses trained to notice.

Autumn's arrival is tricky to discern here in the South,
where trees don't show their cards so easily,
but disguise transformation in muted pastels,
so different from the blazing Technicolor of northern woods
and parkways.

They hide their change so graciously, pretending that life remains
the same.
But, so what if they refuse to release their grip on summer's glory?
I can forgive this denial, knowing full well that transition still
beckons,
and in time, all hands gratefully cease grasping.

Their weakening defiance speaks authentically to my heart.
Deep to deep.
Desire to desire.

Besides, the crepe myrtles are whispering now in burgundy voices
of sweet surrender.

And the sun baptizes their desire in golden choir tones of mercy.

RED LIGHTS

SHERI MALMAN

She sat at the red light and wondered what it would feel like to run it. Straight through. No chance of avoiding the steady stream of SUVs and package trucks and Subarus. She'd lost count of how many times she'd had this thought. And not just recently. For years. *Years*. It wasn't constant or ever-present. But often. She'd never do it. Too much could go wrong. Other people could get hurt. Could die. She could just get hurt. And *not* die.

The light turned green and she eased through the intersection, forgetting she'd needed to turn. Perfect. Her mother's friends referred to these lapses as senior moments. Some of her friends unfortunately referred to these moments as chemo brain. She really had no excuse. Or pithy moniker. Or idea of how to get back home.

First there'd been the annual squish. A few uncomfortable moments in the machine, a few not-so-awkward moments of small talk with the perky PA. Then the call for the call back. And the letter. Another round of squishing. An odd question about a non-existent mole. Another picture. A sonogram. A walk through the rabbit run of offices and file rooms. A semi-secret meeting with the radiologist who only saw the patients who stamped their feet demanding immediate answers. An appointment with a surgeon. To schedule another appointment. For a biopsy. Two biopsies. And then several moments of I-see-your-lips-moving-but-have-no-idea-what-you-just-said.

"So, we'll start the chemo—"

"No, we won't."

"I didn't mean we, obviously. You'll start—"

"No *I* won't."

"I know—"

"No, you don't."

"I don't understand."

"No. You don't."

She flashed back to an unseasonably cold, dreary summer day some thirty years prior when she'd been suspended five thousand feet or so in the air, about to make her first rappel.

"What happens if I don't go?"

"I can't make you."

"I know. But what happens if I don't go?"

"Nothing."

"No really. What happens if I don't go?"

"Then you don't go. C'mon. You can do this. Just push off with your feet. Take your time."

"I don't think I can."

"I know you can. You'll love it. There's no feeling like it in the world. I've got you."

What felt like a twenty-minute conversation back then had probably taken no more than two. She'd pushed off. She'd made it down the several hundred feet to the ledge. There *had* been no feeling like it.

The surgeon, no doubt, like her camp counselor, would be her cheerleader. She'd say she could do this. Could take her time. Would be there—emotionally and medically—on belay. But this was different. If she didn't go she would die. Finally.

She couldn't sort her thoughts fast enough. How did she tell her surgeon that she had no interest in fighting? She was tired of fighting just to get out of bed in the morning. How did she explain more than forty years of suicidal ideation? If this was the hand she was dealt, then this was the hand. She didn't have to inventory her medicine cabinet hoping for the perfect forever-sleep cocktail. She didn't have to pull a trigger (tough to do without an actual gun and zero interest in owning one). Cancer would do the deed for her. And no one would have to know.

"This is a lot to digest. Can I call someone for you? We can push back the start date until next week if you'd like. Let's talk about this."

"Thanks, but no."

"No one to call? I know you didn't list anyone on the records release form, but you can fill out another one."

"No. No treatment."

"Is it the chemo? The side effects? We can keep you fairly comfortable. I know this is scary."

Cancer didn't scare her. Living did.

"That's not it at all. I mean it. No treatment."

"I can't just let you—"

Gathering her things, she stood, opened the door, and with a backward glance assured the surgeon.

"You can, actually. Your oath just says 'do no harm,' right? You're not harming me. Cancer is. And you can't tell anyone. Privilege. It's not just for dead white guys anymore."

Now what? She'd have to get her proverbial affairs in order. At least there were no actual affairs—as in of the heart—to sort. But there was plenty of laundry. And piles. Of mail, of books, of projects. Really? She just found out she's actually going to die sooner rather than later and she's worried about how her house looks? No. She was worried about what her mother and sister would say about how her house looks. After. Such a fine line between wanting to die and being ready to die.

Where was she going? She'd missed another turn.

Last week, she'd felt so decisive in the surgeon's office. But now, home on the couch, abandoned by the dogs that usually hogged the cushions, she reconsidered. Not the not seeking treatment bit. The not telling anyone bit. But sharing the story would mean a confession. Would mean telling.

When had she become so anti-social? She'd taken to ignoring the flashing red message light on both her phone and antiquated answering machine, only sometimes bothering to even look at the Caller ID. Had social media ruined her game? She had gajillions of friends on Facebook. And every time she'd considered spring cleaning her friends list she'd hesitated. She didn't collect friends just to have them. They came from all walks of her life—she'd recognize any of them on the street. But socializing in public had become excruciating. Exhausting. Terrifying. Just getting dressed had become a drama. Having to bathe. And yet, she still managed to put on a public face, go to work, family dinners, occasional social functions. This. This is why cancer didn't scare her. Her life—or seeming lack thereof—did.

Earlier that day, she'd watched, uncomfortably, as hospital interns informed her friend Liza that she would not be well enough to make her family's annual trip. She'd seen the sheet tremble, heard Liza mention, almost casually, that her lips, then tongue had gone numb; that she felt dizzy. A panic attack by any other name. Reality was setting in. And here she sat, knowing that, more than likely, she would find herself in this same situation. Only, she imagined, she'd welcome the news. There'd be no panic. Only more light.

Crossing the acres of hospital parking to her car, she felt dirty. Like a traitor. Like a big capital "L" Liar Liar with her pants on fire. Three hours sitting bedside with Liza, who'd been battling a council of cancers for almost four years. Who'd almost never shown weakness; almost always had a smile, a positive outlook. Who'd never accepted anything but a cure, when no such thing existed. Who'd celebrated three rounds of NED—no evidence of disease—only to find herself in the crosshairs again. A successful businesswoman. Mother. Wife. Sister. Daughter. Who made everyone she met feel like a long-lost friend. Who even now, so much more than the clichéd shadow of herself that barely dented the bed, still wanted to know what books to load onto her Kindle. Who wanted to know if her idea to make donations to the favorite charities of loved ones in lieu of buying Christmas gifts was crazy.

Not. For. Me. I'm not that strong. I'm not that good. I don't have to live for a child. For a spouse. For the greater good.

She had briefly considered reaching out to one of the passel of therapists she'd consulted over the years. But why? She'd dutifully taken what they'd had to say in stride. She heard them all—most of them with the same suggestions—and replayed those conversations. Applied them to her current "situation." No, she couldn't solve the world's problems. Terrible, horrible, no good very bad things happening in other places, to other people, didn't diminish—or invalidate—the everyday despair she felt. What could one of these shrinks say now? Journal every morning? Soak in a lavender-infused tub before bed? Practice meditation? Mindfulness? Yoga? None of that would change the lumps in her breast. Or the lumps in her couch. Or the holes in her heart.

IT had spread. At 3:52 a.m., she had no doubt. *IT* was everywhere. In her brain—on the side that hurt, usually from migraine; in her jaw—that ached from the constant clenching; in her lymph nodes— the flappy bits that oozed from her bra; in her wrist—the one she'd broken as a child—that murmured when the rain came; in her foot— where the bunion had pushed her bones around. Cancer riddled her body. In the blue glow of the telly, she smiled. *Well riddle me this, Cancer. What took you so long?*

As the surgeon drilled and tagged, the sound made her think about how much she hated going to the dentist. And while they laughed about her reference to being tagged—like a pet, or a whale— it made the experience even more impersonal. Perversely, she'd asked to see the specimen. It looked like a zit with a tail, a collection of very large sperm, really. Was there some irony there?

Awaiting her turn in the waiting room she'd entertained herself with how different this would have been with a friend. With Ellie. Who made everything funny. Side–splitting funny. Or with Martha. A bastion of calm, of faith. Her Person. For *those* times. But she'd chosen to go this alone and had to be content with making mental notes. Who was she kidding? She couldn't remember how to get from point A to point B this morning. Rifling through her bag she found one of her trusty notebooks and, eventually, a pen.

Mom and Pop Track Suit with Coordinating Tees. Were they fraternal twins dressed alike since birth? Or a couple together since junior high? The sort that loped through amusement parks in the "I'm His/ Hers" air brushed t-shirts, their hands in each other's back pockets?

Neglected Granny and Caretaker. Both staring at the floor, as uninterested in their surroundings as in each other. Could someone at least have found the woman a pair of matching socks to cover the diabetes–swollen feet, overstuffed into worn plastic slide sandals?

Power Suit iPad-ers. Medical reps? Very Busy Important People waiting on a friend? Rolling Stones. *Tattoo You.* Surely they know where their mute buttons are? Why must we listen to all twenty- seven differentiated alerts?

Please call my name. How much longer? Please. Please. Let's get this over with.

Do we ever experience true silence? Like just–after–the–power–goes–out silence? But that's not silence either, because after a few minutes, moments really, the hands of the kitchen clock have reached metronome proportions. The humming stops during a power outage. The white noise is almost ethereal. Until it's gone. And we begin to hear ourselves. Blood making its way through our circulation system. Roaring through our brains. Is that what we hear when we put a shell to an ear? Just the reverb of our own blood? Is that what Dorothy's red shoes are really all about? Not about *going* home but about *coming* home, to ourselves? We have that connection to ourselves. We don't need to look to the ocean to feel small. Those waves we think we hear when we put a shell to our ear are the waves of life—our own life—coursing through us. And we *are* small. For as closed and tight a system as that of our own bodies, that system, that vast array of arteries and veins and capillaries, all 100,000 kilometers, all 62,500 miles of it, is huge in the confines of a single human. That's five trips between the north and south poles; four around the equator; almost twelve round trips between D.C. and L.A. It's tiny in the scheme of the universe. Call it God, call it Grand Design, call it Evolution. But call it something.

She liked to consider herself a fatalist, forever saying that everything happens for a reason. It is what it is. And yet she'd always struggled with control. Worried about things beyond her control. Reluctant to admit she'd lost control. She'd seemed in control. She'd seemed independent. Sometimes even thought of herself that way. And yet, when the Abyss of depression started to lap at her toes she wanted to relinquish that control. On those occasions, when that tide had come in at her ankles, she'd often relented and let it come to her knees, and then her hips, and breasts, and finally above her neck. Only when it reached her chin, spilling into her mouth, threatening to slip down her throat, to fill her rather than just surround her, had she sputtered and cried, "Uncle."

Martha was her person for those times. And she was Martha's. For more than twenty years they'd mostly managed to just miss each other there, in the Abyss. If one was just getting wet, the other, usually, was just toweling off. Martha was the friend with whom you could break a gym date, but for whom you must answer the phone. Or at least respond with a text or email.

Martha had been the one to fetch her from the emergency room in the early days of her first breakdown. The one to concoct excuses to drop by with "leftover" take–away boxes of comfort food; sit on the couch for countless hours of mindless television and the Sunday *Times*; to check in before bedtime and again after the sun reappeared the next morning. When the worst had passed, she'd extracted a promise. No more deep-end of the Abyss. Don't wait so long. Send up a flare.

In turn, she had seen Martha through family deaths and diagnoses. They'd stood in each other's weddings, navigating the rocky terrain of older brides, spouses with baggage and children. They'd encouraged each other's academic and creative pursuits, strikingly similar in vision and yet characteristically unique in their particulars.

If she were to tell anyone, she'd tell Martha. At the same time, she knew that if anyone would understand why she wouldn't share, wouldn't send this flare, it would be Martha. No. Strike that. Martha would *not* understand not sharing. Martha would be hurt that she didn't trust her enough to count on her saying, "Well, that's up to you. How are we going to get through this stretch? What do we need to do?" Martha would start dropping notes and cards in the mail. She'd put together a basket of treasures and a stack of books— ranging from the creative to the contemplative—and shiny new back-to-school supplies for journaling. And with a Big Gulp of sweet tea secure in the cup holder, she'd hit the road and come to stay. There would be wine. And tears. And more wine. And more tears. And a plan. There was always a plan. Maybe she needed a plan.

Her plan, she'd decided, was to document the plan as it evolved in all its glorious mess. Her final work. Her Life's work. Ok. Her Death's work. She'd try to answer the questions she knew they'd ask. To leave explanations and directives and bequests.

She slowed for the yellow light. Stopped for the red. And thought about this part of the plan. A few cars crossed the intersection. Ok, so she had a grand vision. All her creativity, lost projects, ideas, heaped into one place. A part of everyone who'd made her who she was.

A convoy of garbage trucks trundled through the intersection. No matter that she hadn't managed to finish the last fifteen years' worth of scrapbooks. Had barely cobbled together the wedding album before they'd filed for divorce. Doesn't everyone scrapbook their death? The light was taking longer than usual. Another random selection of cars raced by. Who was she kidding? Already the plan seemed less grand vision and more grand illusion. The light turned to green, and she eased herself through the intersection, not realizing she hadn't done the run–the–light math.

With a rekindled determination, getting out of bed was no longer a chore. She found herself eager to pull on her trainers and walk the dogs not for minutes but miles. Through the woods, across campus, around the lake. No matter the weather. She started cooking again. Really cooking. Not reheating, not microwaving. And while something simmered, braised or baked, cooled or set, she worked on what she'd come to call *The Book of My Dying*.

She tailored two-page spreads to specific people. Tucked in birthday, holiday, and "just because" cards she'd bought but never sent.

Interspersed were the practical pages. She knew many people would ignore the "in lieu of flowers" pleas and those bouquets she asked be delivered to the forgotten in hospitals and nursing homes and neglected cemeteries. She planned her service—her last dinner party, her Last Supper. She included recipes, some passed down, some from the mottled pages of cookbooks, some printed from the Internet. She listed those she wanted to speak or to send something to be read. Chose the songs. She thought about her obit and how she'd never brought herself to draft it. She still didn't know what to say. She added a note to the service page requesting, pleading in her way, for Martha to write it. That moment had led to a bender. A pity party of epic proportions. She had left her bed only long enough to open the back door for the dogs to pee. To refill her glass with either water or wine. She re-watched every episode of *The Gilmore Girls*.

On first glance, the house was messier than it'd ever been. Boxes spilled their contents onto tables and chairs and into the piles. From these she chose the items that decorated the pages of *The Book of*

My Dying. Her books—hundreds of them she'd insisted on keeping after more than a dozen moves, remained on their shelves, sorted alphabetically by genre, by edition, by importance to her—now sported bookmarks with the name of the person or organization to which it should go. She stripped her closets to the bones, keeping only the most comfortable things. Gone were the knee-high boots and the toe-pinching heels. Gone were the sweater sets and silk blouses and suits long out of date, longer still unworn. While the cancer was already keeping its promise to get her back into *that* dress, or *those* pants, she knew she'd soon have no place to wear them. She'd sorted towels and blankets into similar piles for shelters and agencies. And yet none of this made her sad. She felt purposeful. Accomplished. Refreshed.

It'd been a good day. Brunch. Mani-Pedi. Since she wasn't getting chemo, she splurged on cut, color, *and* highlights. She even went shopping. For as much of the last several years she'd spent in yoga pants and favorite faded, unraveling t-shirts, she knew that's not how she wanted people to remember her. She wanted to give her nearest and dearest good last days with her. Of her best her. Funny, witty, put-together her. She was never fashion–forward but she would rarely have made the *Glamour* "Don't" list. Not knowing who'd win the battle between actually cremating her as she was requesting, and burying her according to the tradition of her ancestors—a tradition her family had flirted with in varying degrees over the years—she'd bought an extra white sheet when she'd splurged on a new set for her bed. Albeit still from a discount chain. Even cancer couldn't kill her practicality.

She pulled out of the parking lot and eased into the line for the traffic light. She looked at the dashboard clock and realized that the traffic snarl had something to do with the class change at the university. Six months ago, she would have been beside herself with impatience. Three, maybe four vehicles ahead of her made it through the intersection.

The message light on her phone blinked from her purse. She ignored it and instead smiled at the geese making their way to the pond of the apartment complex on the corner. She could almost sense the impatience of the drivers around her—many with college logo and favorite destination stickers plastered to their back windows and bumpers and gas caps. She saw one driver raise his hand to his horn, pause, and then throw a bird to the geese. She saw several glance up from their phones to see if their status in line had changed, if they needed to bother putting foot to gas. Others turned to their co-pilots in animated conversation. In her rear-view mirror, she saw a car rocking with singing, dancing teens.

Green means go. It wasn't easy being green today. Again, only a few more cars shuffled through the intersection. She had no place to be. No reason to be anxious or to hurry. Bring on the red light. Strains of an old Police tune flitted through her mind. From the *Reggatta de Blanc* album. The car two in front of her slipped in a right turn before the red turned to green for the cross street. As did the next, leaving behind tracks and the unmistakable smell of spent rubber. She looked to her left and saw the traffic snaked for blocks. Not resigned, not restless, but actually content to sit through another light cycle, she fiddled with the radio knobs. Clicked from NPR up the dial through the unfamiliar wilds of Latinx, country, and talk radio. She paused when she recognized the first bars of George Harrison's "Give Me Love," a song that had been a favorite since childhood, an anchor on the first album she ever owned, *The Best of George Harrison*. A song that, even in the depths of the Abyss, reminded her of beauty and joy and good. Of happy.

The light turned green. Again. Finally. Her turn. She'd sat through this light for three, four cycles? And not once done the intersection math. She noticed this time, and took a proud, deep, cleansing breath as she maneuvered her car decisively through the intersection.

MOMMA ON THE LOOSE

MELISSA MCEACHIN

"Anybody listening?"

"Don't think so. I think we're safe," she whispered.

"Honey, you've got a problem," said Madame President of the Gilded Lilies Club, with her dropped chin and glittery reading classes propped at the tip of her nose.

"Duh, I know I've got a problem."

My misty eyes rolled into the back of my head. "She's been standing on my head for days about wanting a puppy. A Goldendoodle, of all things. Her eighty-three-year-old baby sister got one, so she needs one, too.

"Like I need a need another puppy," I sighed. "She *is* the puppy. I just can't take two in the house who need toilet training."

"What's the problem, ladies?" asked the Club's junior assistant as she approached the two of us standing in the corner. Oh brother. That nosy little thing always makes a beeline to any two ladies in *any* corner. You know the type; always right there for anyone in her time of need.

"It's Momma. She's on the loose. She couldn't have gone far except for the fact that she took her purse, her cane, and my car keys."

"And your car?"

"Missing." I began to sob.

"911! Someone call 911!" yelled Junior Assistant as she turned on her heels and ran across the room full of fifty-something gilded lilies. All eyes popped to the corner. Mouths gaping, tongues flapping.

It was time to fess up. I looked up the heavens.

"Momma's gone. Taken my car to who knows where. And with a full tank, mind you. And it's all my fault. My keys," I began to choke, "my keys were next to my purse right over there."

My trembling lips didn't skip a beat as I pointed over to one of the beautifully draped round tables with the hydrangea centerpiece.

"I had to go freshen up, ladies. Nature called, my lips were dry, and I just needed a few minutes in the stall to myself. Surely you understand. Oh, what was I thinking?" I wiped my eyes with my recently pressed sleeve.

Sirens blared as the sheriff's car came up the front drive. Wow that was fast, I thought.

Dragnet walked briskly through the front door, along with Barney, and headed straight to my corner. Dragnet's deep bass southern drawl boomeranged around the room.

"Your momma's been on the loose again. She first made her way to the fire station, where she threatened them within an inch of their lives and then cracked one of the firemen over the back of his head with her cane. She said the next time she called, they better show up." Right about here Dragnet stopped to take a quick breath before continuing.

"The fireman is on his way to the hospital to get stitches. And then," he said with his hands on his hips, "she crossed the street and came right in the front doors of our precinct. She smacked Barney across the face with that dang cane of hers and yelled that the next time she called, we'd better come running."

Now that I think about it, Barney's head did look a little askew.

"This is a criminal case now. That's three times. You know the law. Three strikes and you're out. Come with me."

Barney whisked handcuffs out of his back pocket and before I knew it, I was shuffling down the walk of shame; hands behind my back, steel pressing against my wrists. Umpteen charges surely awaited me. They'd call it elder neglect or some such. I'd call it, "Old woman gone wild."

The women began to tremble and even a few sobs broke through. They all knew the same thing. Today, me, tomorrow, them. They've got mommas, too.

"Where's Momma now?" I whimpered.

"In the clink. Charged with assault and battery. And your punishment, young lady"—the first compliment I'd had in a while—"will be for you to be locked up with your momma until further notice."

"No," I screamed, my kitten heels giving away and landing me on the ground. "Please, no."

Dragnet got right in my face and began to shake me. The louder I yelled, the harder he shook me. I fainted. At least I think I fainted. More shaking.

Wait, you're not Dragnet, you're my husband. What the fire is going on?

"Honey," said hubby. "It's okay. You were having another one of your bad dreams. Now, there." He patted my shoulder gently.

I nodded my head as he left to make the coffee. A dream, it was all a dream. A few minutes later he poked his head back in the door.

"Say, by the way, have you seen my car keys?"

TWO LILLIANS

BARBARA MOSS

My daughter has a second child,
a little girl named Lillian.
She had asked for a list of family names,
and this child is named after my father's grandmother,
known to me only as a photograph
of an old woman in Kansas.

My father says: "She was sure a talker,"
and: "She held her head just so
in every photograph."
Old Lillian's story will soon disappear.
My father is the last link to her, and he is ninety-six.

New Lillian, every part of your story
is in front of you to write.
The only part completed—
you like your mother's milk;
and your father's hands are so competent
as he picks you up and changes your diaper.

Soon you will know the difference between
me and not me,
and the story of New Lillian will begin.

MOTHER MARCH

ROBEN MCKNIGHT MOUNGER

Skidamarink-a-dink-a-dink, skidamarink-a-do, I love you.
—Felix F. Feist

The month of March brings in some rare air. In like a lion, out like a lamb. For me, March cradles the promise of birth and finality of death, highlighted with the dates of my beginning and my mother's passing.

Recently, I officially outlived my mother. At the time of her departure, I considered this day hovering in the future, a possibility not to be conjured. She left abruptly.

Frozen in exquisite detail, I caught up to her and snatched a glimpse of what we would be like as contemporaries, only to have a one-way conversation. As usual, I did the talking.

As I approached her in age, I prepared to close the gap and give her a high five as if to say, "I did it without you, but it was not easy."

The tears have flowed. The elder years that she never lived wait for me nearby. I head for uncharted waters.

During a fifty-seven-year span, we shared the revelry of certain markers: girlhoods in Mississippi, marriages to good men, and devoted children. We are linked by the busyness of daily tasks and the exhaustion that comes from living out of others. Unwilling to move on in a world without the defenses of youth and physical beauty, she unconsciously halted the march of time, but not before passing along some things I needed.

I cling to her distinct brand of intelligence: a curious nature, a desire to make home a haven, delight in the world of miniatures, love of a good story, ambition for handmade gifts, and the proper tools for appropriate dress and good manners to honor the day. For contrast, she lent me a modicum of stormy thoughts and a smudge of the paranoid to frame my hunger for a better world.

These matriarchal gifts often materialize into a scene of mother love. Sitting at the kitchen table, we are eating from bowls of vegetable soup she made. I feel the security of her happy mood as she begins to teach me a song. She insists that I learn each word, as I will have to sing them, on my own, for a lifetime.

Mother-Daughter Vegetable Soup

Vegetable soup was my mother's favorite. I still use her recipe, which, over time, we have consumed in quantity. Her prep included frozen and canned vegetables, all appropriate ingredients for the era in which she cooked. During today's age of farmers markets, I have evolved a fresher rendition. I'm sure Mother would approve this melody.

When the ingredients below are not available, substitute similar types and amounts. You will be pleased with an ever-changing and delicious seasonal soup.

4	purple potatoes, chopped
3	sweet potatoes, chopped
1	yellow Finn potato, chopped
4	carrots, chopped
2	stalks celery, chopped
¼	purple cabbage, chopped
¼	green cabbage, chopped
¼	head cauliflower, chopped
¼	bunch cilantro, chopped
¼	pound spinach, chopped
¼	pound shiitake mushrooms, chopped
1-2	cloves garlic, chopped
1-2	tablespoons miso
¾	tablespoon dried dill
½	teaspoon dried basil
¼	teaspoon ginger, grated
1	gallon water, filtered is best

Heat water and add all ingredients, except miso and cilantro. Simmer on low to achieve the texture you desire. When soup is ready, remove one cup of broth, add miso to the cup, stir until dissolved, and mix back into the soup. Remove two cups of soup mixture with vegetables, blend with blender, and stir back into soup. Stir in cilantro if desired.

BRIMMING EYES, FULL HEART

ROBEN MCKNIGHT MOUNGER

Heaven knows we need never be ashamed of our tears, for they are rain upon the blinding dust of earth, overlying our hard hearts.
—Charles Dickens

Once I gave the eulogy for a man I barely knew. For many years I traded with him on the courthouse steps, where he offered fresh eggs by dint of hens he tended like his very own children. Mr. Malugin's body was found one morning in his vegetable garden, a bouquet of greens still clutched in his hand.

I agreed to his family's request to speak in terms of what I knew about him. He was a poetic figure, but far from personal sentiment.

Pensive enough, I thought, to complete the task, I gazed out from the podium onto those heartbroken faces and a movie of life began to scroll in my head. The script was rich. I cried all the way home.

Six decades were required to take full stock of what I always considered a handicap. Crying is my second language.

As a little one, the propensity sat inside my chest, poised to detonate whether the weather was happy or sad. My mother was scared of it, my father was disturbed by it, and my brother was wary. For a lifetime, I've felt ashamed about my proclivity and either excused myself or choked down the eruptions.

That is until the vibrant Reverend Joe Evans came to the First Presbyterian Church of Columbia, Tennessee.

He lifts my notion of how a person can show up. He proves the ideal that a Christian can be unabashedly enthusiastic about life. And he lives the ancient tribal proverb that says before we can see properly, we must first shed our tears to clear the way.

Our first encounter was at my father's deathbed. Joe offered a fervent prayer, but not without streaming tears. From inside my own house of fear, I told him that it was going to be a long ministry if he gave way for all whom he prayed. He was quick to assure me that there was nothing else more sacred or more proper.

One Sunday as he conducted a service, I saw his emotions begin to rise over the particular blessing of the human condition. As he paused to mellow his tears, he set a tone for the congregation by giving others permission to live a consecrated moment.

From time to time, his forte has included courageous sitting with me and my emotions. Never once did he disturb the trial with words. Healing happened with his empathic presence.

When my grandson Roy cries, his tiny face distorted with emotion, his parents ask what is wrong. He replies, "Me not know." I'm kindred and know his journey.

My hope is that Roy will learn early on, like Joe did, to enthusiastically give way to the beauty of what moves him, whether it be pain, injustice, the majesty of creation, or a good belly laugh.

I once cried for my mother when she told me that she never cried because if she did, she was afraid she would never stop. I'm sure that if she had observed Reverend Evans navigate the beauty of the earth, she would have thrown those chains and let it flow. Let it flow. Let it flow.

Joe Evans is currently senior pastor at First Presbyterian Church Marietta in Marietta, Georgia.

Spring Rolls

Joe loves to plant a few vegetables and herbs each year. When the basil is ready for harvest, he whips up a batch of spring rolls. He passed along an inexact rendition, because spring rolls are a matter of favorites. You can develop your own combinations after some practice. Chopped beef, chicken, shrimp, or tofu can also be added. Amounts of each ingredient will vary according to taste.

1 package spring roll skins
1 package rice vermicelli noodles
1 or 2 jalapeno peppers, seeds removed, finely minced
1 bunch of basil, chopped
1 bunch of cilantro, chopped
1 or 2 cucumbers, thinly sliced
Rice vinegar
Hoisin sauce and/or thai chili sauce for dipping

Add enough rice vinegar to cover thinly sliced cucumbers and set aside. Prepare rice noodles according to the package. Drain. Heat a shallow pan of water to just below boiling. Take one spring roll skin and submerge it for thirty seconds or until soft. Remove it and place the smooth side down and the rough side up. Layer noodles, jalapeno peppers, cucumbers, basil, and cilantro along the bottom of the spring roll. Begin the roll from the bottom and roll, first turning in the right side and then the left side. Continue rolling until the filling is used up.

Dip rolls into desired sauce before taking a bite. Smile.

1967

CINDY PHIFFER

The congregation had already sung the first two songs, and Elmer
was leading the opening prayer when Odell Denny came in. He
walked to the next-to-the-last pew on the left and seesawed his way
to the farthest end of the row.

Eleven-year-old Mary Anne saw this through squinted eyes. *Same
overalls*, she thought, and turned her head in time to see Aunt Ina
craning her neck to check him out. Uncle Elmer wound the prayer
to an end about that time, with a request to "Bless Brother Benton
as he brings us the lesson," asking this "in the name of our Lord
and Savior, Jesus Christ, and Amen." Several men added their own
"Amen" while Uncle Elmer returned to his seat next to his wife.

Brother Arnold rose from his front row seat, took a quick look at
his watch, and turned to face the congregation.

"Our song before the lesson this morning will be number three
hundred," he said, then repeated, "Three hundred." As books were
grabbed and pages turned, Brother Arnold began to sing, holding
his book in one hand and pumping the congregation to life with
the other.

It took one whole line for the sound to rise from a moan to a
chorus in four parts, where the singing began in earnest. Preacher
Benton Way's booming bass provided the bottom line, four altos
followed Sister Ina's braying, Elmer's trembling tenor found its way
through the middle, and everyone else sang the melody led by Sister
Opal's warbling soprano.

Mary Anne sang the words by heart, watching her great-uncle
Arnold beat time with a motion that looked like squeezing a blood-
pressure bulb. She was lolled into a sort of hypnotic state when
suddenly the song ended, and everyone settled into their seats.

"The song of encouragement will be number two-hundred nine,"
said Brother Arnold. "That's two-oh-nine immediately following the
lesson." He lumbered to his seat next to his Ina, and turned his eyes
toward the podium.

There was much shuffling as books were marked and slipped into the backs of pews and fans were pulled out. The preacher slowly stepped up onto the podium, wiping his mouth with his hanky. Brother Way arranged his Bible just so on the pulpit, straightened his string tie, and cleared his throat. Finally, he lifted his eyes to the congregation, which had settled into an expectant hush.

"First," he said, calling his meeting to order, "let me say that we're mighty glad to have my wife back with us." Two of the older men said "Amen" to that, and Mabel Taylor reached up to pat Opal on the back. Ina, seated on the row in front of her, reached back and patted her sister on the knee.

"We thank the Lord for her speedy recovery, which has enabled her to be back in our midst." Brother Benton didn't have to explain further. Everyone at Bent Creek knew about Opal's headaches. If it weren't for Dr. Estes's willingness to make house calls, Opal would have been in and out of his office more often than Mabel Taylor, who was a hypochondriac before anyone in Middleton knew there was a word for it.

"I'd also like to express our heartfelt thanks to our Sisters Bea and Elna." Each reached into her purse for a tissue. "This lovely bokay," he said, gesturing toward the flowers on the stand in front of the podium, "was given in memory of their dear, departed brother Philip." Bea sniffed and Elna blew her nose.

Mary Anne watched all of this from where she sat with her friends in the last row. This was an important day for her. She had decided to be baptized, so she tried extra hard to pay attention. But when Elroy wrote the word *fart* on her back with his finger, she was distracted for several minutes, trying her best not to laugh.

"...and that's why," her grandfather was saying when she turned her attention back to him, "we won't be meetin' here for the reg'lur Sunday evening service next week so we can all go over to Slippery Rock. Their Gospel Meeting starts next Sundy mornin' with Brother Medley a-doin' the preaching. I think most of you know Brother Medley, the daddy of our very own Elmer Medley." Benton looked up to see most of the audience nodding. Brother Medley had moved to Detroit to preach the gospel when his son was just a baby. Two of his brothers and a cousin had followed him, looking for work in the booming automobile industry. Although Brother Medley lived there still, he returned to Middleton once a year to preach at his home church's homecoming service, which ended a week-long revival.

"He's done some mighty fine work with the boys at the Preacher's School up north, particular in the area of the Great Commission." Brother Way paused again, checking to see heads all over the room bobbing their agreement, then he continued. "Now if you would, turn in your Bibles over to the book of Ephesians, chapter 4 and beginning in verse 4."

Brother Way waited as Bibles were rounded up and pages fluttered. When the noise died down, he read, "There is one body and one Spirit, even as ye are called in one hope of your calling; One Lord, one faith, one baptism, one God and Father of all, who is above all, and through all, and in you all.

"Now, I have selected this passage this morning to get us ready for some good lessons on the Great Commission by Brother Medley. As you know, we were commanded in the Great Commission to 'Go ye into *all* the world, and preach the gospel to *every* creature. He that believeth and is *bap*tized shall be *saved*; but he that believeth *not* shall be *damned*,' Mark 16, verses 15 and 16.

"Some of our brethren over in Piney Woods has decided that," and without missing a beat, Brother Way's voice turned surly and mocking, "why, we don't need to send *our* hard-earned dollars over to foreign lands to preach the gospel. It's a waste of *our* money," he smirked, "to send missionaries over to places where they already have big fine cathedrals to worship in. We should just send them to countries that don't have no religion a'tall." Eyebrows raised nearly to his hairline, Brother Way paused before returning to a seriously grave tone and bent closer to the microphone. "Brothers and sisters, I tell you this is *blas*phemy!"

This time, several of the men said, "Amen."

Brother Way, looking satisfied, stood straight again, and went on. "Going back to the passage from E*phe*sians, *Je*sus said in plain English, there is only *one* church and only *one* way to get into it, that being baptism. Now, since we who are in the *Lord's* church have been blessed by being brought into the Lord's *one* faith by holy baptism, it is not only our de*sire* but rather it is our solemn *du*ty to take the message of the hope of that salvation to the unsaved *all* over the world. A*men*?"

"Amen," the men echoed back obediently.

Brother Way allowed a moment for effect, then lowered his voice to give himself room to swell. "Now there are men that think they are saved. Ye-e-s," he said, drawing it out like taffy, "they sit in their big church-houses and they sing along with their big fancy organs and, why, they might even *tithe*." Several of the young children giggled at the thought of an instrument in church, and none of them had ever heard the word "tithe," so that was funny to them too, especially the way the preacher's lip curled when he spit the word out. The irreverent kids were swiftly shushed or smacked on the back of the head by the adult closest to them.

"But brothers and sisters, Satan is playing a cruel joke on them." The fifty-five-year-old preacher went into a rhythm of his own as he picked up steam.

"That's *right*, the Devil his*self* has them fooled into thinking they will be among the hundred and forty-four thousand headed for a home in *glory*. But Jesus said," holding his Bible high in the air, "right here in the Good Book, that if they are not washed in the *holy* waters of *bap*tism, 'they are like the chaff which the *wind* driveth away.'"

Odell, silent and still, grinned. *There he goes again*, he thought, *taking the scripture out of context. The chaff thing was from Psalms, written by David a long time before anyone had heard tell of baptism.* Odell's head shook slightly. *Course, not one of them reads their own Bibles enough to know the difference. Just take his word for it.* Odell chuckled, drawing disapproving glances from the women. *And they think I'm the one who's foolish.*

Brother Way was getting wound up. His face was flushed and he nearly bounced as he spoke. "Going back to the lesson from last Sundy, the Bible *clearly* states that we must follow *all five steps* if we are to enter those pearly gates on the day of atonement." He held up five pudgy fingers in front of him.

"First," he said, pulling his pinkie down with his other hand, "we must *hear* the word, Revelations 2 and 7. Second," pulling his ring finger into his palm, "we must be*lieve*, Acts 16 and 31. Thirdly," pulling his thumb in and leaving his pointer and middle fingers up in peace-sign fashion, "we are to re*pent* of all our past wrong-doings, Acts 17 and verse 30. Fourth," pulling his middle finger in, "we have to con*fess* for 'with the mouth confession is made unto salvation,' Romans 10 and verse 10. And last, but by no means the least," he shouted, "the *one* way," thrusting his upturned pointer finger toward the ceiling, "to assure an eternal home in *glory* is to be buried in the waters of baptism as we are com*mand*ed in John 3 and verse 3."

As Brother Way had increased in fervor, the congregation stirred with an electricity that caused fans to fly, heads to nod, several to say "Amen" some to say, "Um-hm," and others to say, "*Yessir.*"

Odell shook his head imperceptibly. *There he goes again, putting words in Jesus' mouth, he thought. John 3:3 says that Jesus said, "Verily, verily, I say unto thee, Except a man be born again, he cannot see the kingdom of God." Oh, sure, he goes ahead to explain that being born again means being 'born of water and of the Spirit' in verse 5, but not in verse 3.*

Brother Way, feeling the people in the palm of his hand, suddenly dropped his voice to a hush, as though he was sharing a big secret. His eyebrows danced.

"If our Lord had'a meant for us to go around sprinkling or a-throwing water on poor, innocent babies, don't you think he would'a said so?" Turning up the volume a notch, he said, "If he'd of meant that it was alright with him for us to just *say* we believe, don't you think he would'a said so?" Bea nodded and rocked. Brother Way took a sip from the small glass on the pulpit and kicked it into high gear.

And even louder, he said, "And if he had thought that it was ok for us to divide his holy church into the many denominations that are in existence today, *don't you think he would'a said so?*"

At once, his eyebrows ceased their aerobics and Brother Way returned to his normal speaking voice. "The facts is that *Jesus* never said any of that. He made it clear, folks, plain and simple. If you don't want to spend eternity in the fiery depths of hell, you must trust and obey."

Mary Anne had gotten her first spanking for not sitting still in church. Now she felt as though she was frozen to her seat. Her heart was racing and her grandfather's words had her scared half to death. She hoped she could stand up when the time came.

Brother Way wiped his brow one more time. "We're goin' to sing a song of encouragement," he said, and the congregation put their fans away noisily and pulled out the songbooks from the wooden slats that hugged the backs of the pews. Brother Way droned on in sing-song rhythm, raising his voice to be heard over the sounds of the congregation, many of whom were already thinking about what they were having for lunch.

"If you have not accepted Jesus Christ as your Lord and Savior, *now* is the accepted time. Harden not your hearts. Open the door and let him in for to*day* is the day of salvation. Tomorrow may be too late. Won't you come, as we stand and sing."

On the upbeat, Brother Arnold started singing "Just As I Am" as he took his place at the left of the Lord's Table. At the same time, Brother Way came down and stood in front and to the right of the table, holding his Bible and searching the congregation, pleading with his eyes.

During the first couple of verses, Mary Anne glanced around nervously. She waited until her heart was beating so loudly she could hear it over the singing, then she leaned into the aisle and headed toward the front. She was met with a firm, warm handshake and a half-hug by her grandfather. The singing grew softer as the women dropped out to weep. Bea glanced back to share the moment with her thirteen-year-old son Dilton, but saw at once that he, too, was headed down the aisle.

Oh, thank you, God, for bringing my children unto you. Mary Anne is a good girl and she'll work hard in your kingdom. Dilton, on the other hand… well, You know. Bea thought all of this without missing a single word of the invitation song.

As the song ended, everyone sat down and several men wiped their eyes with hankies pulled from back pants pockets. Brother Way sat down next to Mary Anne and put his arm around her. They whispered for a minute, then he whispered something to Dilton before standing and turning to face the members of Bent Creek.

He wiped his eyes with his hanky and said, "You know, every baptism is special. But today, I have been asked to do the honors for my own grandchildren." Ina snuffled out loud and Opal patted her on the back. "Mary Anne and Dilton Thomas come this morning confessing their sins and expressing the desire to turn away from the evil ways of the world and walk in newness of life, choosing as their Master our Lord and Savior, Jesus Christ, by being buried with Him in the holy waters of baptism." Turning to face Mary Anne first, Brother Way grasped her right hand with his and put his left hand on her right shoulder.

"In accordance with His commandments, Mary Anne, do you believe with all your heart that Jesus Christ is the Son of the living God?"

Mary Anne's soft voice nearly whispered, "I do." Several women cried audibly.

He repeated the process word for word with Dilton.

"The angels are rejoicing around the throne, for two lost souls have been brought into the fold." Brother Way hugged them both, then with his arm still around Dilton, he headed toward the door to the left of the podium. Mary Anne, her mother Bea, and her Aunt Elna went through the door to the right.

Brother Arnold returned to the front and announced the first of several songs they would sing while preparations were being made for the baptisms.

As soon as the door shut behind the ladies, Bea and Elna wrapped their arms around Mary Anne and squeezed until she thought she might pass out. Then they went to work, pulling a baptismal robe and three towels out of the cabinet under the sink.

Bea shook the garment out, and grabbed it by the hem, gathering it up toward the neckline. As Mary Anne stepped out of her dress and handed it to her aunt, Bea slipped the baptismal robe over her head.

Meanwhile on the other side of the building, Brother Way shook Dilton's hand, then handed him a baptismal robe and a towel. Dilton stepped into the stall and closed the door behind him. While he changed, his grandfather stepped into his rubber waders.

It had been a while since the little church had a baptism, but the familiar feeling of joy and pride washed over the preacher. He hung his string tie and watch on a peg on the back of the men's room door, then put his suit coat on the same peg. Next, he took one step back and sat down on a folding chair to take his shoes and socks off. He did all of this without thinking. It was part of who he was. Rolling his sleeves up to his elbows, his mind wandered to the big lunch that always followed a baptism. He hoped Ina brought her rolls. They went so well with his wife's chicken.

Dilton slowly opened the door of the stall. Brother Way said, "Come on, son," and opened the side door, which led out into the baptistery. He motioned for Dilton to wait just inside the door. Brother Benton got down the steps and halfway across the chilly water before Mary Anne appeared from the other side. He met her eyes, saw that she was ready, reached out his hand and steadied her as she stepped into the water.

She flinched as her foot touched the water, but she clenched her jaw and continued toward her grandfather. She hadn't expected the water to be cold, and her mind wandered. *I hope I don't get water up my nose.*

The preacher in his rubber suit guided the young girl to a spot directly in front of him and turned her around to face her mother and aunt who were waiting with towels at the top of the steps. The congregation started into the third verse of "Trust and Obey" as Brother Way whispered instructions to Mary Anne. He placed a folded handkerchief in her hand, and reminded her to take a breath before covering her mouth and nose. Brother Arnold stopped the singing at the end of the chorus, and stepped aside to watch the baptism.

With his right hand on her back, Brother Way raised his left hand and closed his eyes. "I now baptize you in the name of the Father, the Son, and the Holy Ghost. Amen." With that, she brought the hanky to her face and slowly laid back. In two smooth moves, down and up, the baptism was complete, and Brother Arnold immediately started singing the first verse of "Oh, Happy Day" over the sound of a choked gasp and the slosh of long hair and heavy cotton coming up out of the water.

Mary Anne waited at the top of the stairs while the congregation finished the first verse. She wanted to see the baptism with her own eyes. It was something she had always prayed for, but now she realized that she never really believed it would happen. *Oh, me of little faith,* she thought, scolding herself.

As Dilton was lowered into the water, he talked to God in his mind. *Now, we're even.*

Mary Anne followed Bea and Elna back into the bathroom. She peeled the wet things off, while the two older women dried her. They even held her clothes out for her to step into. Mary Anne felt fresh and new inside, and she could tell by the look on Bea's face that her mother understood.

Brother Benton and Dilton returned to their seats in the front row almost immediately. By the time the women slipped back into the service, Brother Arnold was leading the third verse of "Break Thou the Bread of Life." During the singing, Elmer and James came up and stood at either end of the communion table. Each took hold of the white linen tablecloth at each corner with their thick workman's hands, lifted it, and stepped in front of the table in one movement. Together, the two men folded the cloth, handling it as reverently as they had folded the flag draped over Brother Benton's daddy's casket.

James stepped back behind the table, clasped his right hand with his left, and let his arms hang like weights. He picked a spot on the back wall and focused on it. As the song ended, Elmer carefully set the folded cloth on the corner of the table.

In silence interrupted only by an occasional cough, the Lord's Supper was served. Elmer lifted the lid from the top bread plate, placed the lid on the table, lifted the top plate, and bowed his head.

"Our heavenly Father," he prayed in an unnaturally loud voice, "we thank Thee for sending Thy son Jesus to die on the cross for our sins. As we break this bread, may we do so in a manner that is well-pleasing to Thee. All this we ask in the name of Thy Son and our Savior, Amen."

A hushed "Amen" came from the men of the congregation and the room fell silent once more. Elmer handed a plate to James and took the other plate himself. Elmer waited while James served the folks on the first row. Dilton broke off a piece of the bread that was far too big. Embarrassed, he shoved the whole thing in his mouth and passed the plate to his sister.

The unleavened bread looked like a huge cracker marked with a grid. Mary Anne pressed down on the cracker with her left thumb, and broke off a tiny square with her right before passing the plate and popping the bite of "the body" into her mouth.

James and Elmer walked toward the center aisle and each of them started his plate down the next row, Elmer to the left side of the aisle and James to the right. As the plates moved away from the middle, Elmer and James stood solemnly still, hands folded in front of them, and watched the plate make its way down the first row. At the end of each row, the last person turned and handed the plate over the back of the pew to the person behind them. It was a procedure that had served the congregation well, and would no more be altered than the order of service.

Most of the adults kept their eyes squeezed shut and their heads bowed until the plate reached them. Then, they opened their eyes and broke off a small piece. After placing it in their mouths, they returned to their meditative state.

When James and Elmer reached the last row, they walked back up the center aisle together. The shiny metal plates were stacked together on the table and covered with the lid. Next, James removed the lid from the top tray on the right, lifted it slowly with both hands, and bowed his head.

"Our most gracious heavenly Father," he mumbled quickly, "we come before Thee, thanking Thee for this fruit of the vine which represents the blood of thy Son and our Savior, Jesus Christ, shed on the cross for our sins. May we take it in a manner that is well-pleasing to Thee. All this we ask in Jesus' name," and this time he left the Amen to the men of the congregation.

The entire procedure was repeated, this time with the small glass cups being placed into their holes on the pew backs. So far, Mary Anne's first Lord's Supper was going as she had hoped. She was so afraid that she'd spill the dark, purple juice down the front of her dress that her hands shook. She crossed her fingers for luck as she reached for her first drink. After successfully maneuvering the cup, Mary Anne let out a sigh of relief and passed the tray on down the row.

When the men returned the trays to the Lord's Table, Elmer reached underneath the table and pulled out two straw baskets with flat bottoms covered with red velvet. Handing one to James,

Elmer said, "Let us return a portion of what we have received, remembering that the Lord loveth a cheerful giver."

When the baskets were returned to the shelf under the table, Brother Ben led one verse of "Blest Be the Tie." James stepped into the center aisle and faced the congregation, their books returned to the backs of pews and their heads bowed, awaiting the closing prayer.

"Before I lead us in dismissal," he said, pausing to clear his throat as one by one, people peeked up at him, "my wife and I would like for you to come to our house for dinner followin' the service. Let us pray. Our Father who art in heaven, go with us now into our respected places in life. Guide, guard, and direct our steps and if it be Thy will give us a home in heaven in the end with Thee. In Jesus' name we pray, Amen."

TO BE A GROWN-UP

MARY MARGARET RANDALL

My summer was dramatic. And I am not one for drama. Too much stress, never enough rest. Too many speeding tickets, never enough patience. Too many days forgetting to eat lunch and ribs poking out through an already thin body. Never enough time.

Too many days without yoga, too many scheduled commitments. Too much worry and anxiety about the outcome of a relationship I had spent years pouring my heart into. Never enough Solitude, Creativity, or Self-Care.

Let's be honest: If I had known twenty-nine would have been this challenging, I would have skipped straight to thirty. I am beyond tired. I am tired of performing. Tired of doubting. Tired of making decisions. I am tired of convincing myself that I am worth the pursuit of romantic partnership.

My handprints are forever marked on the spotless aquarium glass, just gazing hopelessly into the forever blue. So much envy and longing to be free in the deep water—away from this land, away from overbearing feelings, away from all things human.

What happens when you want time to stop but it doesn't? What happens when you don't want to grow another year older because you are scared of the weight of expectation that comes with it?

I feel like a child begging to stay home from school. *Please God,* let me stay as far from responsibility as possible, where I can keep my head eternally buried below my favorite yellow comfort blanket, the one I clung to in small, quiet corners in my Alabama home. The blanket I liked to pretend was my personal cocoon, where my feet were always warm and I was embodied in the softest wool imaginable, and I was *protected*.

No one told me how hard all this would be, to be a grown-up. No one told me about the pressure you feel to figure out your life, to make good money doing something you care about, and that you could in fact feel that pressure every single living day, like a second layer of skin wearing you down.

No one told me about the marathon run of finding a life partner and then, like miles of muscle soreness, the aches and pains of getting him to stick around.

No one told me about the piles of bills that show up at your house uninvited. Worse than guests who wear out their welcome. Worse than the neighbor who never leaves.

No one told me you might lose all dignity the moment you start crying after countless attempts to upload an electronic signature on a pdf file, feeling that the computer has outsmarted you for the hundredth time this week, despite the fact that you are a borderline millennial and you should know these things by now.

No one told me how vulnerable and scary it is to start a business on your own and that you might just second-guess every single minor, meaningless detail to the point of paralyzing every ounce of creativity you have left in your bones.

No one told me how hard it would be to go to weddings—not all the time, but some of the time, enough to dread the invites.

If you had asked me in college what I thought twenty-nine would look like, I would have said, "Oh, maybe kids, marriage, a small house with a dog."

This is funny to me now, peculiar even. It is true: I used to think of marriage like a license plate. It defined who you were and it was expected for every Alabama southern belle from Gulf Shores to Huntsville. And you couldn't make it too far on this so-called road of life without this important little tagline. Why of course, you *had* to have marriage to be anyone important, to be anything close to a respectable, sophisticated young lady. Otherwise, you might get pulled over by the officers of the faith who stand there and look you in the eye with their arms crossed and eyebrows low, to give you a warning and a deadline.

I feel sorry for this young naïve version of myself: that I would give marriage this kind of power, that I would put so much blind faith into this manmade identifier. For me, it was always about this romantic, playful fairytale where the girl gets her prince. But does every girl even want a prince? And is life really that simple for everyone?

Understanding adulthood sure has taken a lot of un-learning and re-learning and then un-learning again. I feel like a kid on a playground figuring out how to jump rope—each jump getting more and more complicated, knowing there might be a few skinned knees involved.

Growing up means stepping into the unknown. It means taking risks and moving forward even if you are not a hundred percent sure of what's next, because truth is, no one is.

Growing up means peeking my eyes out from under my comfort blanket and then slowly but surely, my nose and mouth too, until finally, I lift my stubborn head into the cold room entirely, greeting the day in all of its newness.

Growing up means being honest. It means admitting your mistakes. It means asking questions when you don't know how to do your taxes. It means speaking your loneliness out loud.

Growing up means taking dance lessons even though it costs money. It means forcing yourself to sit down and write a poem before dinner because you're afraid of what will happen if you don't. It means looking a child in the eye and seeing heaven. It means taking walks outside in the quiet underneath a blanket of trees with no cell phone in your hand and nowhere to be.

This is what growing up means to me. I know it's not perfect, but it is something. And that's all I can do right now.

CONVERSATION WITH RAYMOND CARVER'S "AT LEAST"

SHARON REDDICK

Sometimes even modest dreams
are too much in which to hope.
But sometimes to move
from sorrow to living dreams
is simply a matter of moving
from bed to writing desk.

Put your feet on the floor.
Maybe the hour is cruel and cold,
but put your feet on the floor.
And rise. Break it down to that.

Then channel yourself
from a time when walking forward
wasn't hard—when you were eight
and you had a best friend
down the block, or sophomore year
when all your classes were across campus.

Use your muscle memory from those days
and move your feet across the room.
Then sit down at your desk by the window,
watch the waves break on the rocky beach,
and take up your pen.

SANTA FE, SEPTEMBER

BARBARA RUSSELL

After the Drought

Rain
slices through melon sky.
I swear
I heard the arroyo laugh.

Sunset

The old plaza
stands silent
as evening arrives
in its gray shawl
rimmed in gold.

YELLOW OLDS

BARBARA RUSSELL

Safe within your yellow Olds
we sped home that August night:
black dairy farms against navy sky,
Catskills ahead
the Mohawk River tilting south
toward the mighty Hudson.

"Hey Jude" came on the radio,
And despite the dash's eerie glow,
you let me listen.
Silently, I broke away
dreaming my dreams
(mostly boys and clothes at fourteen)
as you kept steady at the wheel.

The night got darker;
we'd put off leaving—
one last swim
getting the cat in.
Besides, you knew this route
from twenty years' practice.
I was your last child
and only girl,
both boys now launched
Dad settled at last.
You shared your stories
in a smoke-filled haze;
my role, just to listen
and remain unfazed.

But sitting side-by-side in that creamy car,
I dreamed my eighth-grade dreams.
Elegant, even powerful, you and that Olds
took us home
that August night
and four or five more;
but our bond was fraying
my need for you waning.

As our headlights hit the Kingston Bridge
and the Hudson's fog enveloped the car,
we left that summer
and that childhood
on the darkened bank.

OUR BOY

ALAN STALLINGS

Carrie Ann and I had been told that if our son, Alan, survived two years from the end of chemotherapy without evidence of return of the tumor, then we had "a chance" of a cure. By the end of August 2006 we had reached a hopeful milepost. It had seemed like forever.

Alan had gone through six months of inpatient treatment that included huge surgeries, as well as multiple rounds of chemotherapy and radiotherapy, at Children's Hospital of Philadelphia. We lived in an apartment near the hospital for a year as he finished his chemotherapies. He had not suffered a recurrence. Although his speech was improving, his swallowing was not. But with the gastric tube feedings he looked healthy and had in fact grown in both stature and weight. His mind was better than ever. And then, best of all, it was time to leave the Philadelphia apartment and return home to Jackson, Mississippi.

Our struggle was far from over, but things were better. Carrie Ann was able, finally, to relax a bit, a state that does not come naturally to her. It is difficult to explain the depths of her dedication and intensity, as well as the fact that for the seventeen months in Philadelphia she did the work of at least two people. Probably closer to four.

The weather had been particularly nice for the last month or so; the trees had the most brilliant fall colors in years; the sky was a fabulous Mediterranean blue; and the temperatures and humidity were nearly alpine. Or was it that we finally lifted our eyes high enough to see the trees and the sky, to enjoy the sunshine while it lasted? We had not had that luxury for a while.

Alan went back to school a couple of days after he returned, and his first report card was Bs and As, which seemed barely short of incredible. Academically, he didn't scrape along but excelled. Given his absence, surgeries, chemotherapies, and radiation, we had worried, and been warned, that any, and all, of them could decrease his intellectual ability. They didn't. A great part of this was because he loved school, his classmates, his teachers, and learning itself. He smiled both going to school and coming home.

Because he was still unable to swallow much, his G-tube pump ran all night. He ate with everyone else, chewed and enjoyed the taste and texture of the food. He reported "some" progress in his swallow, but it was slow. The day when the G-tube could be discontinued was still far away.

Fourth grade revived all of our spirits. Alan blossomed as never before. When he first returned he was a bit ill at ease; partly from his previous absence and partly from the necessary apparatus that he brought with him. The halo was the most impressive and obvious difference, but the feeding pump that he now wore clipped onto his shirt and the G-tube were the more delicate and, to the casual observer, more mysterious. Ever secure in who he was, he quickly warmed up to his classmates and they to him. He sometimes used the halo as a prop, and in his music class would do a robotic dance. It was not long before a couple of his classmates helped him fill the feeding pump reservoir.

His strength returned in increments, although he still tired easily. The third Saturday he was home, the two of us camped out in the backyard for the first time in a long time. Slowly, ever so slowly, we returned to some sense of normalcy, though we never forgot what lay ahead. It would be years, perhaps as many as five or six, before anyone might assure us that the cancer would not likely return. In the meantime, we hoped he would either re-grow the bones or have a cervical fusion for stability. It would be great progress to get out of the halo apparatus.

Our adventures improved; we went from backyard camping to fishing to hunting. Both of us enjoyed being outdoors, and because Alan had spent so much time in confinement, he had a special appreciation for being outside.

We went to baseball games. Alan loved fireworks, and always insisted that we stay until the fireworks at the finale. We took a metal detector and did amateur archaeology in the yard. We went to church.

Alan's sense of humor was unchanged. Never one for pranks or practical jokes, he was more inclined toward intellectual reflection than slapstick, more infected with critical nuance. While it was always on our minds that this strangely behaved and deadly tumor might return, we reveled in our activities. We threw birthday parties and holiday parties and parties for no reason at all. We went to restaurants.

The academic year was one of wonder and of grace, and Alan was amazingly cheerful. And he fully deserved to be. In light of the horrible conditions of the past several years, this was heaven. No shots, no radiation, no chemotherapy; just family, friends, and fun. Best of all, a greater measure of regularity in our lives.

Alan was never a discipline problem. Rarely corrected and rarely punished ("Go to your room and sit in a chair" was the worst punishment he ever received). That did not change in this remission. No bad behavior. None. No compensation for past difficulties. No explosions of temper. No whining for reparations for what he had been through. He sailed along. His mature personality allowed him to find life grand and full of joy. I had known others who had escaped difficult times who seemed to feel a newfound freedom after the episode was past. They had gotten used to the special place and favors shown to them, and expected them to continue; they often became irritating. Alan never exhibited the first hint of that. He had such humble strength that all he wanted to do was blend right in. He never sought privilege because of the hardships he had endured. It reflected his strong, quiet character.

The one area where Alan was limited was in physical activity. He would never ride a horse again, never sit behind me on the motorcycle, never pedal a bicycle. We cautioned him to use extraordinary care to climb the steps to the tree house. He was so sure of himself that we did let him swing. We feared any substantial fall, even in the halo apparatus, because his neck lacked the support of a normal neck. Not that it stopped him from anything. His teachers kept a close eye and often pulled him out of activities they thought too physical. And he would push the limits set for him. Just his nature.

It was a time of peace, as if we had come inside out of a blizzard and were exhausted, but warm and dry. We basked in family togetherness, doing daily tasks, reading, talking, breaking bread. It was golden. We played games, we went to museums, we slept late.

Carrie Ann and I both kept the possibility of a recurrence close to the surface of our thoughts. Perhaps even this added to our enjoyment of this time, the added edginess and risk. But it was a time of solid enjoyment and we appreciated it. Alan summed it up beautifully: "It is just so good to be home."

We had already made arrangements with a local funeral home. Carrie Ann did not want to have him taken out of the house on a stretcher, so I carried him to the front porch and placed him on the stretcher. Then they took him.

Both of us wanted him cremated since his poor body had suffered so much. Carrie Ann arranged the memorial service, which was held the next week. Ann Walt, our daughter, and I contributed little except to insist the service begin with Bach's "Toccata and Fugue in D Minor." This complicated, difficult piece is one we had played occasionally for our children, with an admonition that it should be how you live your life. It is solemn, heavy music, which gives way to majestic beauty. If you are unfamiliar with it, pull it up and listen to the version played by E. Power Biggs. You may have to listen to it more than once to fully enjoy it and absorb its power, but it is a worthwhile nine minutes. At the recessional, a bagpiper led us out and played "All the Saints." Friends came from Philadelphia, Atlanta, Oregon, Los Angeles, and Little Rock.

For quite a while after his death, we were numb. Despite knowing full well for months that the end was coming, it did not feel right. It did not feel real, despite the struggle being over. Our son had lost and had died. Carrie Ann was exhausted to such an extent that even recovering her sleep would take weeks.

Slowly we began to come back to life. As always, reflections of the weather seemed more important than they probably were. A beautiful end to a beautiful day. Clear blue skies. Temperature in the seventies. Calm wind. Alan's dog, Herman, sat next to me; a dove and a mockingbird flew through the yard. Neighbors walked by on a gorgeous day. Cricket song.

All was perfect, except Alan was not there. I gazed across the courtyard to the place where he died. The pain of his absence persisted. The tears persisted. When would they diminish? Would they diminish? I missed him desperately.

There seems at times to be a surreal quality to sudden death, sort of a cognitive dissonance. Someone was alive yesterday or last week, today gone—killed by some sudden and unexpected cause, say a heart attack or car accident. It is difficult to conceive at times; it seems not possible. Our minds like habit, like status quo, and we expect yesterday to be the template for today. Even with Alan's long battle with cancer, his death had a surreal quality—probably related to our intense involvement in his care. We had much difficulty accepting the obvious. It simply wasn't supposed to be.

During his epic battles, we had enjoyed many victories—some of them great and seemingly miraculous. There had been a relative absence of defeat. Sure, he had been badly wounded, but he was still with us, as was his enduring desire to live. We tried to face the death of our son, our boy who loved trains and art and the moon and birds and science and school and his dog. And most of all, his family.

We gave all we had.

We never told Alan to "be brave." We did not need to. His bravery buoyed us, made us braver in the face of disaster, of his demise. His courage and determination seemed greater than ours in every situation.

We have been left hollow and empty from our loss. Life, and what it means, have pivoted dramatically. Carrie Ann said few things matter now that aren't a matter of life and death. We still enjoy quality: food, friends, travel, music, museums, and learning. The frills, though, are immaterial. At times we see people who grouse about trivial things. Things like being in a hurry, having their meals prepared exactly as they wished, waiting on transportation, or worrying about their dress or appearance. We look appreciatively at each other and think, *If you only knew how unimportant that is.*

In the evening, about the time of Alan's death, I become more sensitive to surroundings. A distant train whistle to the northwest brings another wave of memories; another flood of tears. Even the sound itself makes me miss Alan terribly. Maybe I will re-read Lamentations.

We keep Alan's toys as portable, miniature reminders. For the first year or so, Matchbox cars and trucks sometimes fell from trees where the squirrels have taken them. Apparently the squirrels have a taste for the tires as the vehicles fall with their tires chewed off. His room is still filled with completed Lego projects, as well his books and his "healing-drum" and telescope. But we do not enshrine the artifacts of our son's life; we have used the room, used his telescope, just as the squirrels have used his Matchbox vehicles. Almost every day I drink coffee from the Amtrak mug Alan proudly presented to me in the Philadelphia train station as I left one evening to return to Jackson. The mug has survived so many cycles in the dishwasher that the lettering is now faded. As I drink from it, the memory of his handing it to me, smiling, inevitably comes to mind. The objects we keep are themselves without value, except as repositories of his memory.

Because of Alan's intense interest in geography, we have also honored our boy by taking some of his ashes to places he wanted to visit. We have done this as a family.

On the whole, Carrie Ann and I have dealt with grief in different ways. Perhaps it is a reflection of our ancestral genes, or our earlier lives, or our gender chromosomes, but she has told me (repeatedly) that at times I expressed anger and she did not.

Neither of us blamed God. The experience has not made me question my faith. In fact, while I have become less involved in organized religion, I feel more spiritually alive than before Alan's illness. After all, while the eventual battle was lost, as it shall be with all of us one day, there were so many situations where Alan beat the odds, had so many seemingly miraculous recoveries. Who is to say those prayers weren't answered? My own feeling is we were blessed beyond belief and, of course, beyond anything we deserved. We attend church less than in the past, but pray more.

We have so many joyful memories. We hope with time those will remain and the bad memories, the memories of pain, illness, failure, and defeat will leach into the shadows of the past.

Most of the time between diagnosis and death, we flew by instinct, taking some clues from our surroundings and those leading us, not unlike Virgil leading Dante through hell. And we certainly went through hell, and not all of us came out. But, again, like Virgil, we were shown great kindness and graciousness and sympathy and especially prayerful support from so many people.

Some people can bear acute pain, while others run. You realize there is no magic that will lift it from your shoulders. Instead you hope it will abate with time. As we have passed the ten-year mark, we have all shown some improvement but so far only minor. Understandably, though every day brings this pain to our minds, some days are worse than others. Holidays, birthdays, and anniversaries are especially hard. We try to concentrate on the good times.

Sometimes this itself is painful. I remember many of our happiest moments during this difficult time. Partly because it was of a long duration, but mostly because it was a time when we were so aware of the likelihood of the loss of our son, we were tighter knit, unified in purpose, and realized we should enjoy life when and while we could. As far as life itself goes, we are all only temporary custodians of our physical shells. We are only stewards of our possessions and of life itself. And it is over all too soon. In the end, all fades, all vanishes, except faith.

A BONDED LAMENT

EBONI WEBB

I chose him under an indigo moon
A season of impenetrable blue
Scarcely seeing or feeling
the depth of this misstep
Blind to his wounds
I settled deep with salted tongue
and acid tears
Praying for salvation
and broken redemption
it was my season of running
an imprisoned break from life
my leap over an abyss
beckoning me home
So, I leapt as he held
clasp turned to grip
grip to clamp
clamp to lock
lock to vice
Oh God, what have I done?
Longing for a moment
with my grandmother
reviled by her betrothed
How did you endure?
I judged you water weak
not understanding the strength of floods and waterfalls, and
tsunamis
Grandma I hurt
Grandma I'm falling
Grandma I don't know what my hands look like anymore
Pain changes child
Falling ends
and hands are shapeshifters
Open them to hold your heart, child
Close them to receive no more
Cup them to embrace the worthy
Flatten them to stand
On your feet, child.

BONE OF MY BONE

EBONI WEBB

I found myself in your gallery
Dark mass, unstructured, formless
Stealing an outpouring of iron and bone
Your undoing
My becoming
Twisting I came into this world
Pushing
with your bones

Encircled in your warmth
I am found in your soft cage of flesh
Sweated, stretched and tested
Enmeshed

One Flesh
One Bone

Bones hardened with age
Throw words without care
Over your shoulder
Now mine

Mirrored cheeks shine with tears
Flowing rivers on the same path

I found you again in your
Now brittle gallery
China-Bone weary
Enfolded in your frame
One more time
Our frame
My undoing
Your becoming
Untwisted
Cage-less
Free.

COMMON TO UNCOMMON GROUND

EBONI WEBB

A wide set nose and a broken taillight
Brought a young man to a common grave
Haunted with young men with names like Emmett and Trayvon
Daughters, lovers, and mothers wail anew at nothing new

Rape and a blue-eyed witness in a ghetto gentrified
Brought an immigrant to an uncommon grave
A fiancé, a distant continent at the bottom of the world, and mothers
wail at something new

Blood spilt unwarranted and forbidden
No complexion protected
All victims
A world unborn,
guided by ghosts

African-American

Native America and Africa.
Two mothers collided-shared birth—
Spilt blood on stolen earth.
Fighting, shackled, tongue-broken.
Families divided and reunified
Hues and textures stripped and blended in every new eye and
foreign color
Our women spread
Carrying that which was both ours and not ours.
Birthed songs of struggles, a new gospeled jazz,
Rich as our native drums and origin stories.

Our men,
forced to dream of leadership without authority
finding power in submissive resistance.
Veins filled with faith, tears, and fire.

Our story became the story of others,
Touching, tormenting and tickling
rumors, lyrics, and laments.

We were hidden in riverbeds
Or brazenly swinging high in willow trees.
Full of tongue-swollen prophecies

We paid
To have sound connected to words,
to worship a God of choice,
to earn a hyphen
on this terra that we have called home.

MONA

AMY LYLES WILSON

Mona set her fisherman's basket purse—a gift from her late husband, Ernest, during that last trip to Maine—next to her lawn chair, which she had dragged out of the potting shed after reading in the *Grace River Junction Gazette* that the Glen Miller Orchestra would be playing over in Luckettville City Park. If she timed it right, she could grab an early lunch at the Lunchbox before driving the fifteen miles. Luckettville got more concerts and had better shops (don't tell Estelle at the consignment boutique Mona said that) because they could claim a four-year university there, and a decent hospital, not just a community college and a walk-in clinic like here in Grace River Junction. At least that's way the mayor, Ed Henley, put it during his most recent "State of the Town" episode on the radio as a way to explain why we continually get passed over for such events. Ed liked to consider himself a twenty-first-century version of an admired historical figure giving a state of the union address. His citizens did not hold him in that kind of esteem—no "Fireside Chat" reputation—but no one else wanted the job of mayor, so unless the roads were impassable in the winter or the farm animals got loose during the annual parade, the fine residents of Grace River Junction tried not to complain too much.

After making sure Hiram was settled in his crate and the house was locked up tight—Mona never had believed in leaving her doors unlocked and after her neighbor had his garden hose stolen last month she wasn't going to start employing blind trust in her fellow man at this stage—she put her reusable tote-bag from the library book sale in the backseat of the car and headed out. She had put a water bottle, some tissues, hand sanitizer, and an apple in there just in case. You never knew when you might need to blow your nose or stave off hunger while you were on the road. At the last minute, she also threw in her old stadium blanket, the plaid one, in case there wasn't room for her lawn chair and she ended up having to sit on the ground. She hoped that didn't happen, because these days, at her age and all she'd been through, there was no guarantee she'd be able to get back up without assistance. And Mona hated asking strangers for help. She didn't even really like to ask her children or her friends from church for assistance, but an old lady simply needed a hand now and again. Like the time the light went out over the kitchen sink and Mona was scared to stand on the little stepladder without someone to spot her. She was just healing up after her hip replacement, so thankfully Carl from the hardware store hadn't minded. At least he had said he didn't, and Mona was inclined to believe him, seeing as how she had never had occasion to doubt him before.

Mona and Ernest had been friends with Sally and Carl for more than forty years, from back when they were all young and their kids were in school. Mona wonders sometimes how she even survived being a mother, that's how nervous she was about the whole process. She wasn't tough, she didn't like confrontation, and she often had to lock herself in the bathroom so her children wouldn't see her crying after one of them had slighted her with some offhand comment or refusal to do what she had asked. Ernest picked up the slack, though, being happy to play the role of disciplinarian, leaving the softer roles, like comfort and cookie baking, to Mona. That she could handle, as she'd been trained at the feet of Big Mona, who was considered the best hostess in all of Grace River Junction at one time. It might not sound like much to you, but it said something about how Mona and her family were regarded—at least at one time—in the community. Reputation mattered to Mona, and even though she was in her twilight years herself now, she didn't want to do anything to sully things. Why risk it? That's why when she took off for the concert, she made sure she was smartly dressed—white chinos, cotton blouse with little sailboats on it, a short strand of pearls, and her favorite Merrells.

Sometimes Mona wished her fashion choices had more flair, like those of her friend MayBelle. (Mona is fully aware that other people in town would use a different word to describe how MayBelle dressed.) But Mona never has been one for colorful shawls or dangling earrings.

Should she take a hat with her to the concert? Probably not, given the five p.m. start time. And anyway, she had just gotten her hair done and she liked the way it looked, even though it was thinning now. She had stopped coloring it years ago.

"You shouldn't stop dying your hair," Ella had said. "It will wash you out too much, Mother. You're already so pale, like me."

It was true. Without extra rouge and bright lipstick Mona and Ella were both pale as starched sheets. But that's where Mona drew the line since turning seventy. She was tired of paying extra for the color, and it never looked quite natural anyway. The few times she had done it at home herself, with a kit, it was a disaster. And there were stains she still couldn't get out of the towels she used, even after multiple washings. She'd taken to using them to dry off Hiram after he'd splashed in the creek on their evening strolls.

There was a bigger crowd than usual at the Lunchbox, but Lonette, the owner, waved Mona over to a small table in the far right-hand corner.

"Sit," she said. "I'll get you some silverware."

Mona knew what she wanted, of course, for she always ordered the same thing: salad medley plate with chicken salad, egg salad, and pimento cheese. Congealed salad and blueberry muffin included. If Doc Delaney were to wander in he might try to lecture Mona on her eating habits, but seeing as how her blood work from her most recent physical showed normal cholesterol and blood sugar levels, Mona figured she was in the clear. Sometimes Mona allowed herself sweet tea, too, but today she decided on water. Something had been keeping her up at night, so she thought she'd try cutting back on the caffeine to see if that helped.

By now, she ought to be able to eat whatever in the heck she wanted. She couldn't live forever, and with the way things were going in the world these days she wasn't even sure she wanted to live through the concert. Oh, of course she enjoyed her children and her grandchildren, her volunteer work in the community, and her gardening, but seriously, who would want to be young today with all the crime, political upheaval, and downright degradation in society? It was enough to depress anyone, and it often depressed Mona. But she was trying hard not to let it get her down. Instead she was trying to focus on the positive things in her life.

One of those positive things had come as quite the surprise, right out of the blue. When Carl had come over to help with the light in the kitchen a couple of weeks ago, he lingered a little longer than usual—a little longer than was absolutely necessary—before leaving. For a minute there, at the door, Mona thought he might be about to kiss her on her right cheek. Goodness knows they'd both been lonely since losing their spouses. She turned away before embarrassment could overtake them, but she must admit it had fired up a little spark. He had called the next day to invite her out for lunch, but she had already been planning to work her shift at the library so she demurred. She hoped he would try again.

After circling the parking lot near the city park, Mona spied a spot where she could slip her old Volvo wagon in without much trouble. She had to be especially careful when driving, so as not to get in an accident or damage the car. She knew she'd have to give up the keys eventually, and she didn't want to be one of those old people who waited too long to make necessary adjustments. But so far so good: no traffic citations, no fender dents, and only an occasional honk or raise of the middle finger directed at her by someone in a hurry, usually someone who appeared to be about twelve years old and over-indulged.

She was beginning to make her way to the bandshell, having gotten her provisions out of the car and slung the chair over her shoulder, when she thought she heard someone calling her name. She stopped, briefly, and, not hearing it repeated, kept moving.

"Mona, wait up!"

There it was again. She stopped and turned halfway round, only to see Mattie Banks lumbering toward her. My, how she hated that woman. Mona knew you weren't supposed to hate, that the Bible advised against it, that her mother had taught her better, all those things. And yet. Mattie Banks. You'd loathe her, too, if you knew her.

"If I'd known you wanted to come to this I would have asked you for a ride," said Mattie, panting. *If I'd known you wanted to come,* thought Mona, *I'd have hidden in the crawl space under my house.* She was afraid of that crawl space, as full of slithering and smelly things as it was. And still, she'd rather be there than here, with Mattie Banks. *God forgive me,* she thought as she picked up her pace.

"I only decided to come this morning," said Mona. "No time to call around for carpooling."

"I thought for sure someone would invite me to go with them," said Mattie, adjusting her bra strap. It was a washed-out color, not nude or ivory, sort of grayish, really, and wider than most.

"But everybody I tried said they had other plans. Funny, I thought the senior center might get a group together."

Mona knew for a fact that the senior center did indeed have a group coming. She'd been tempted to join them but preferred to have her own car so she could leave if the mood struck her. She'd always been that way, prepared to exit at a moment's notice.

"Well," said Mattie, oblivious to how disinterested Mona was, "at least we can sit together."

Mona had no intention of sitting with Mattie, but she'd have to come up with a reason why. Mona was pretty good at thinking on her feet, and she'd have to prove her mettle today. Maybe she could go to the bathroom and then head in a different direction, giving Mattie the slip. Mattie wasn't too bright, so it shouldn't be too hard.

"Where do you like to sit? I have to sit close so I can hear," said Mattie. "I've got some hearing aids—my daughter made me get them—but I don't like to wear them." For a few seconds Mona thought Mattie didn't even know she was there. She might be able to walk off right now, while Mattie was blathering on, and Mattie wouldn't be the wiser.

"I have to sit farther back..." said Mona, lying. "I do have my hearing aids in, and if I sit too close the feedback is bad. So maybe we should just sit on our own." Mona starting shifting away from Mattie as she said this.

"Oh," cried Mattie. "I don't like sitting alone with all these strangers." By this time they had made it to the band shell. Mona had already picked out a good spot and was eager to get settled.

"You'll be fine," said Mona, turning toward her spot. "We'll compare notes afterwards."

As Mona heard the first sounds, she looked toward the tree line and saw the group from the senior center. She loved some of these people, she did. But she was glad to be right where she was, taking it all in on her own. Mona, for one, appreciated the long view. She liked to see the forest *and* the trees whenever possible. Today she had a view of it all: the band shell, the crowd, the food trucks, and the craftspeople who had set up around the perimeter. She realized she was hungry, even though she had eaten all her lunch, including the grapes, which she usually didn't bother with. If the food trucks where still there when she left she might treat herself to something for dinner. She could take it home and warm it up, that's what she could do.

Once, at a street fair, Mona had sampled some of the food trucks and been quite impressed. Some of her friends had stayed away, talking about sanitary food practices and all sorts of potential digestive maladies, but Mona had eaten and lived to tell about it. She was learning to live a little. She had quite enjoyed her veggie wrap, truth to tell. Maybe today she'd try a quinoa bowl.

Soon after the orchestra started playing "Moon River," Mona heard the woman next to her say, "Sterling. You remember dancing to that at the Crystal Palace?" Mona watched as the woman squeezed her companion's hand. And then Mona started to cry. She hadn't meant to, of course, didn't really care for public displays of emotion. But if Mona had learned anything since Ernest died, it was that there was no accounting for grief. It hit you when it hit you, and you best just ride it out.

AFTERWORD

The door is open and the coffee is hot.

"Tell me," she said. "What are you doing here?"

The weather was bad, so she thought no one would come.

"We wouldn't miss it for the world," we said, wondering how she could not know that. Her husband and dog have been ousted from our creative space, leaving us blissfully to ourselves to apply the pick and shovel to long-hoarded miseries and triumphs.

Our seats at the table provide us with a safe place to unravel the secret threads of our pasts, weaving truth with fiction. Each session involves uncovering what's real, discarding the unnecessary, and refusing to allow the truth to stand in the way of a good story.

The table is large, and surrounded by willing participants. This willingness is not always entered into easily, though, or casually. Generally, at some level, there is purpose involved. A creative catharsis, a need to express, a desire to discover, an ache to explore and share the interior self in the company of supportive souls.

Each person is fully present. Each individual opens up to the flow from within. Funny, profound, mysterious, painful. All is welcome here.

Together, we walk through the valley of the shadow of death that leaves us panting in anguish, as well as through the mountain-top experiences that allow us to see into our own future. Possibilities poke their heads up like daffodils in a March snowstorm.

So what happens when the final bell rings, and the group disperses? Each of us goes our separate way, and all looks the same as before. But it is not. For in that chunk of time spent together, hearts and souls have been bared; laughter and tears, breathless amazement, have been shared. Each writer gave birth to new thoughts, words strung together as never before. All present shine the lights, hold them up, say "Yes" and "Amen" to each other.

We leave feeling heard. Empty of regret, and hopeful for what is to come.

—Cece DuBois and Cindy Phiffer, longtime Pilgrim Writers

CONTRIBUTORS

Sherry Vance Allen lives and writes in Birmingham, Alabama. She has spent her professional career as a communicator, but through Pilgrim Writers has learned how to communicate in a different and more meaningful way. She expresses her creativity through writing, cooking, and interior design. She is a lover of dogs, nature, golf, good food and drink, and truth. Her daily goal is to live up to the Kipling quote, "To meet with triumph and disaster and treat those two imposters just the same."

Linda Barnickel is the author of the prize-winning *Milliken's Bend: A Civil War Battle in History and Memory* (LSU Press, 2013). She usually writes historical nonfiction, based on extensive research in primary sources. She joined Pilgrim Writers during its first year and uses the group's meetings to expand her writing repertoire, working in formats that continue to stretch and challenge her and provide greater opportunities for creative learning and freedom.

Thomas (Tom) W. Campbell, M.D., is a psychiatrist/psychoanalyst in Nashville. Although loosely based on real experience, his piece is a work of fiction.

Julie Cantrell is a reformed chemical engineer and late-bloomer in the world of creative endeavors. She left the corporate world for a second career in the nonprofit sector. Now retired, Julie hopes to spend more time writing and pursuing all the creative things she never had time for before. Although she can still whip out a mean Excel spreadsheet, her main love is sitting down with a blank page and a fountain pen.

Stephanie Cenedella is a writer focusing on advocating for communal conversations where everyone gets a seat at the table. She is in the final stretch of completing her memoir, *Daughter's Truth*. Snapshots of her story appear on www.honorthygayfather.com. Her essays have appeared in *The Gay Dad Project*, and at the *Chautauqua Institution's Literary Arts Summer Series*. Stephanie resides in Boulder, Colorado.

Lisa Dammert is a nature lover and poet who is perfecting the art of picking herself back up and writing her second act.

Cece Dubois is a writer—of prose, verse, and song—who also paints portraits, builds furniture, and renovates houses. She sings, acts, laughs, and prays. She's a designer—of interiors, wardrobes, and ideas—who intends to live out the rest of her life doing these things as big, as often, and as loudly as possible. If she sees the end approaching, she'll do it faster. www.cecedubois.com.

Susan Spear Dyer was born and reared in Richmond, Indiana. She has found a life in Nashville, Tennessee, for more than forty years. Susan is a seeker of all things beautiful and authentic. She currently works as a resident chaplain at St. Thomas West Hospital, sharing the thin, transitional spaces with those she serves.

Karen Fentress is a poet and artist who makes her living as a lawyer in Nashville, Tennessee.

Ami Fletcher received a bachelor of science in agricultural education from Western Kentucky University and studied theology at Vanderbilt University Divinity School. She received her certificate in spiritual direction from the Haden Institute, and has a spiritual direction practice in Springfield, Tennessee. Her practice also includes grief counseling and life coaching. She is a licensed minister with the Christian Church in Tennessee (Disciples of Christ). Ami started journaling at the age of twelve, a practice that continues to serve her well now that she's in her fifties. She enjoys taking creative writing classes, and she's also a musician who pursues her passion through a community choir.

Mandy Ford is an artist and higher education professional living the small-town life in Indiana with her husband and twin boys. She has a knack for finding beauty in the small things, a ridiculous amount of hope, a child-like fascination with life, and is in a serious relationship with her morning coffee. You can find out more about Mandy at www.mandyford.co.

Eve Hutcherson is a native of Kentucky who lives in Nashville, Tennessee, where the city's vibrant music, arts, and creative community provide ongoing fuel and ideas. Her current work, published regularly on The G-ma Chronicles (www.gmachronicles.com), is a light-hearted look at changing roles for today's grandparents, ever-shifting family dynamics and aging, and mid-life issues for women. Eve has worked as a journalist and magazine writer, publishing in regional, national, and international publications for more than thirty years. Her work has earned awards in both news and business competitions.

Janis Lovecchio is ever fascinated with manifestations of the sacred that appear in the natural world, in ordinary life, and in the stories we tell. She finds great comfort and endless possibility in silence, solitude, and walks in the woods. Janis is employed by Holy Family Catholic Church in Brentwood, Tennessee. She serves in a wide variety of roles, her favorite being that of a spiritual companion and receiver of the sacred stories of others.

Sheri Malman plays with words for fun and for hire. Armed with more than twenty-five years of publishing experience and a master of arts in English, she supports both emerging and accomplished authors, teaches reluctant college writers, and helps civil servants polish their prose. www.sherimalman.com

Melissa Davis McEachin used to buy large spiral notebooks as a child in Jackson, Mississippi, with the hopes of filling them up with stories. Now she's finally doing just that. A graduate of the University of Mississippi, she and her husband, John, have lived in the Nashville area since 1991 and have an adult son. She helped develop and produce a musical for Kid's Evangelism Explosion, *The Big Trip*, and has worked with the Nashville Choir on several projects at the Schermerhorn Symphony Center.

Barbara Moss is a lawyer who like to writes things other than briefs and contracts. She has won a number of awards for legal knowledge and community service, but considers her most important awards a kind husband and six lovely grandchildren.

Roben McKnight Mounger has lived her life primarily in Mississippi and Tennessee. Intermittently she has traveled to other places. She is devoted to cooking with local ingredients for all peoples and occasions. She is a storyteller who cherishes the ability to illuminate the wizened and the newly born. You can find her at www.mscookstable.com.

Cindy Phiffer is a prolific writer who enjoys experimenting with a variety of genres as much as she loves exploring the arts from music to painting to collage. Her ability to write rhythmically turns her prose into a near-poetic form, and she treats her realistic characters with transparency and empathy. Born in Detroit, Phiffer considers herself Southern by heart, a fact that makes her writing sing.

Mary Margaret Randall has been writing, a little too inconsistently, for a consistent amount of time. When she moved to Nashville in 2010, she started a blog (aheartthatsmiles.blogspot.com), and it is there that she found her authentic voice. Mary Margaret blends personal storytelling with metaphor, often told through the lens of nature. She enjoys working with children, teaching yoga, and developing her nonprofit organization, One Voice Nashville, which teaches middle- and high-school youth the art and craft of storytelling and narrative journalism as a way to build bridges and close gaps in the community.

Sharon Reddick is a poet and a lawyer, not necessarily in that order. It depends on who's asking. By day, she works as an assistant district attorney prosecuting child abusers. Evenings and weekends, she watches hockey, practices yoga, occasionally cooks meals for her family, and writes poems. She has been a grateful participant in Pilgrim Writers since 2013. She lives and writes in Nashville with her husband, son, and two dogs, one of whom thinks he's a cat.

Barbara Russell grew up in upstate New York and graduated from Northfield School and Wellesley College. She has taught Spanish and worked in publishing. After marriage and a move to Nashville, she has worked as an editor and translator. She began writing memoir and poetry in 2011 and has read for the Tennessee Women's Theater Group and Scarritt-Bennett Poet's Corner.

Alan Stallings, M.D., graduated from Hendrix College and the University of Arkansas Medical School. He taught at the University of Mississippi Medical Center and worked mostly in obstetrical anesthesia. He enjoyed the practice of medicine, including medical mission trips to both Guatemala and Haiti, retiring in 2014. Passions include sailboat racing, scuba diving, and flying planes; just about anything outdoors. He has fly-fished and hunted around the world. His work has been published in medical journals and wildlife magazines. Stallings lives in Jackson, Mississippi, with his wife, Carrie Ann.

Eboni Webb is an entrepreneur, amateur cook, and novice writer. She's a sucker for a tragic story, and passionate about advocacy for the marginalized. When she's not catching up on sleep after a week of delving deep into the stories of the broken, she's likely binge-watching *Game of Thrones*, *Better Call Saul*, or pining for *The Handmaid's Tale* to return. She was "accosted" in a parking lot by her friend and inspiration, Amy Lyles Wilson, to join her Pilgrim Writers group, where she rediscovered her love of writing poetry and storytelling. She is forever grateful to have been pulled from the daily minutiae to a table of amazing women writers.

Amy Lyles Wilson is a story coach and spiritual director who founded Pilgrim Writers to help people tell the stories they need to tell. She has co-authored or contributed to eight books, including *This I Believe II* and *Bless Your Heart: Saving the World One Covered Dish at a Time*. Her work has appeared in a variety of publications and on National Public Radio. She holds degrees in English, journalism, and theology, as well as a certificate in spiritual direction from the Haden Institute. She is a trained affiliate of Amherst Writers and Artists, and has served as adjunct professor and writer-in-residence at the Earlham School of Religion. She leads workshops across the South and at the Chautauqua Institution. www.amylyleswilson.com